I ONLY JOINED FO

I ONLY JOINED FOR THE HAT

REDOUBTABLE WRENS AT WAR
THEIR TRIALS TRIBULATIONS AND TRIUMPHS

CHRISTIAN LAMB

Bene Factum Publishing

Published in 2007 by

Bene Factum Publishing Ltd
PO Box 58122
London
SW8 5WZ

Email: inquiries@bene-factum.co.uk

ISBN: 978-1-903071-15-1   (1-903071-15-1)

A CIP catalogue record of this book is available from the British Library.

Printed in Malta.

Cover design by Paul Fielding, London SW15 1AZ

Edited by Liz Cowley & Auriol Griffith-Jones

Designed by Prue Fox of Donough O'Brien Consulting, London SW15 1PW

Cover photograph of Wrens tricorne hat courtesy of the Imperial War Museum

To my husband John

In appreciation of the part he plays in this book
and how much he would have enjoyed it

CONTENTS

———— ⚓ ————

LIST OF ILLUSTRATIONS

———— ⚓ ————

FOREWORD
by
Countess Mountbatten of Burma CBE

I am of the same generation as the author Christian Lamb, with a very similar career in the WRNS, and her story took me back over 60 years to the three happy years I spent, aged 19 to 21, in that service from 1943-1946.

This book gives a real flavour of the amazing variety of work undertaken by Wrens - from routine and mundane to highly responsible and dangerous. But whether working at a desk, in a canteen, in an engineering yard, with little boats or employed on secret information, the girls always worked with a high sense of duty and of 'doing their bit' to help win that terrible war.

Looking back from such a long 65 year vantage point, it strikes me anew what an extraordinary experience that time was, leading from the complete security of early youth into a totally different new world of excitement, danger, boredom, fear, exultation, apprehension and battered emotions of all kinds. But above all, what shines through in one's memory of those extraordinary days is a shared sense of purpose and determination in the face of great difficulties.

I think those of us of that generation who survived the war were really lucky to have shared that sense of purpose and a uniquely bonding experience between strangers which served us all very well for the rest of our lives.

Patricia Mountbatten of Burma

INTRODUCTION

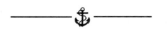

The idea of writing this book came from a dinner party last Christmas, when I must have been expounding on some Wren story; Diana Luck, a friend and neighbour I have known on and off for years said, 'Why don't you write it all down?'

I immediately wondered if I could, and knowing Diana had been a Boating Wren, asked her if she had ever recorded her own experiences. She had, and there and then promised to dig them out, if after so many years she could find them. Diana duly unearthed her memorable contribution and included some contemporary letters she had written to her parents, which all appear as the book proceeds. This flying start gave me the idea of writing down as much as I could remember about the highlights of my own war service (1939-1944), bolstered by firsthand accounts from other ex-Wrens, who had been in unusual and interesting jobs or who had stories to tell. The main challenge was how to seek them out, now that we were all well into our eighties. To add to my book, these redoubtable ladies had to be a) alive, b) willing and if possible c) compos mentis, not by any means a given among us ancients.

So here will unfold the splendid firsthand accounts of unsung heroines, some never before related, many of them written off the cuff at my request, some more sophisticated than others, but all in their own inimitable style. A few are extracted from their books, or the *Wren* magazine and all are interwoven with my own recollections. There will be a lack of consistency in the chronology of the narrative as I cannot always remember what came first.

One aspect of this plan was quite unexpected and I was amazed how bereft I felt when in trying to contact some of my contributors, discovered they had died. Having got to know and like them through their inspirational writing, it seemed tremendously nostalgic that I was to be deprived of the opportunity to thank them in person and exchange memorable instances of our lives so long ago. Communicating with those of our dwindling band has been a rare treat, finding we are still much of the same mind, ready for anything and especially to renew or make a friendship and to indulge in comparisons of our ancient and modern lives.

Christian Lamb

ACKNOWLEDGEMENTS

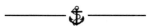

There are a great many people to whom I owe a debt of gratitude, and the first is to Countess Mountbatten of Burma whose foreword launches this book at the rate of knots.

I particularly want to thank my contemporary Wrens for their contributions. In alphabetical order: Catherine Avent, Daphne Baker, Freda Bonner, Mary Brown, Sheila Carman, Maria Chaworth Musters, Jean Cochrane, Betty Cruddas, Mary Earl, Lita C Edwards, Jane Fawcett, Ruth Joly, Anne Glyn-Jones, Joy Hale, Priscilla Hext, Mary Hilton Jones, Hazel Hough, Fanny Hugill, Sister Pamela Hussey, Molly Jenkin, Mrs Graeme Laing, Diana Luck, Hope Maclean, Monica McConnell, Phil Murray, Elizabeth Duchess of Northumberland, Philippa Roberts, Margaret Shooter, Lady Kenya Tatton-Brown, Baroness van Lynden, Norrisse Whitehead and Mary Wynn-Jones.

I have used, with their permission, some brilliant extracts from the following books which greatly add to and illustrate my narrative: Patrick Beesley - *Very Special Intelligence* and *Very Special Admiral*, Bernard Fergusson - *The Watery Maze*, FB Hinsley & Alan Stripp - *The Code Breakers*, Audrey Johnson - *Do March in Step, Girls*, Angela Mack - *Dancing on the Waves*, Lady Rozelle Raynes - *Maid Matelot*, Commander Ryder VC - *Combined Operations 1940-1942*, Nancy Spain - *Thank you – Nelson*, *The Wren* magazine...and especially Lieut Commander John Lamb DSC - *Tales of the Last Dog Watch*.

Acknowledgement and thanks are also due to: Candida Balfour, Giles Clotworthy, Jean Davidson, Prue Fox, Biddy Graham, Auriol Griffith-Jones, Nick Laurie, Colin Macmillan, Alan Mason, Donough & Liz O'Brien, Mike Phillips, Audrey Urion, Anthony Weldon, Lady Westbury and Dr Colin White.

CHAPTER 1

DOING ONE'S BIT

A figurehead is variously described as 'a carved and painted figure on the bows of a sailing ship or as a decorative emblem on the bowsprit or beakhead of a vessel, which has ornamental value but is of no practical use'. This sprang to mind as I sighted the remarkable female who greeted me as I set foot in the foc's'le of the first Wren establishment I joined. Her name was Hilda Buckmaster, who in her youth was known to have sailed before the mast in a windjammer - a splendidly over-endowed woman with a well established tophamper and rough bluff cheeks. She greeted me, leaning forward from her large kneehole desk, almost endangering her embonpoint, with these enthusiastic words. 'How nice to have to welcome a breath of fresh sea air!' I wasn't sure whether she was referring to my father's Admiral status or my slightly rolling gait. I had been to a rather good lunch party, and for a frozen moment I wondered if she was going to offer me a pink gin. I was reminded of the famous cartoon, which depicts a twelve year old hopeful cadet at his interview for the Royal Naval College at Dartmouth.

I had travelled back from France by the last ferry across the Channel just as war was being declared, and not having

EXAMINING ADMIRAL (*to naval candidate*). "Now mention three great admirals."
CANDIDATE. "Drake, Nelson and—I beg your pardon, Sir, I didn't quite catch your name."

opened a newspaper for about six months, I was much more taken up with the French family life from which I was being wrenched. There, I had been totally absorbed in becoming bilingual, reading all the riveting French novels which had been banned during my previous life at my English convent school, in between falling in and out of love (in French of course), and was not at all in the mood to pay any attention to this inconvenient war.

The author

In this frame of mind, I travelled up to Scotland to stay with my mother and schoolboy brother, who were sheltering there with my grandmother; she had the most heavenly house at Speanbridge, near Fort William, where my sister Anne and I had always spent our school summer holidays. Now I had to concentrate on a correspondence course with an Oxford don who would tutor me through the Latin exam necessary for entrance to Oxford, where Anne was already reading Philology. I sat the exam in solitary state at the Fort Augustus Monastery, invigilated by Benedictine monks - I must admit to being distracted by the scenic view of Loch Ness where I hoped to spot the monster - many of the monks claimed to have seen it.

By now of course I had read the papers, and it was quite obvious that Oxford was not an option until the war was won, and that one must choose some way in which to 'do one's bit'. I thought of becoming a VAD, (Voluntary Aid Detachment); the initials rang a sort of Florence Nightingale bell, prompting me to fit First Aid lessons in between the Latin, and my step-grandfather nobly allowed me to practise 'capillary bandaging' on his rather bald head - as if a green first aider would ever be allowed anywhere near a patient requiring such a bandage. However, when it came to the idea of dealing with stumps, I quickly realised nursing was not for me.

My grandmother had not only arranged for her chauffeur to give me driving lessons, but was also teaching me to play bridge, and one of her friends who came to be a fourth at the game, was a Colonel Frank Laughton; (once, when he and I were playing together we made a Grand Slam, seven No Trumps, doubled and redoubled, which as anyone who plays bridge will know is a tremendous excitement.) As luck would have it, Frank's sister Vera Laughton Mathews had recently been appointed Director of the Women's Royal Naval Service, and almost her first inspired act was to employ a top designer to create a uniform, based on that of the WRNS in World War 1 (in which she was just old enough to have taken part) and which included the splendid tricorne hat. I had always been extremely hat-minded, and even at the age of three had evidently admired and insisted on copying the Prince of Wales' hat adjustment, when I was taken to the station to see him arrive by train. What could be easier than to persuade the Colonel to write me a reference? This I duly enclosed with my application form to join the WRNS and sent it off.

It had never occurred to me that there would be officers and ratings, as in the Royal Navy, so it was a surprise to find you had to start in the lowest rung of the ladder, equal to ordinary seaman. After an interview and medical examination, preliminaries which took place in London at the Wren Headquarters over Drummonds' Bank beside Admiralty Arch, I was closely questioned by a senior Wren Officer called Nancy Osborne. 'Have you any qualifications? Can you type?' Unable to boast of any such merits, she nevertheless seemed to view me with favour, and said there would be a vacancy for which I could apply at the WRNS HQ if I failed to be accepted for anything else.

I could not imagine I would ever contemplate working in such a place surrounded by old biddies; my ideas were much more romantic. I was joining up to free a sailor to join the Fleet, but had expected plenty more of them to be around to lighten one's heroic endeavours.

The medical was quite straightforward, except for the moment when the doctor was testing my hearing. I had rashly confessed to a mastoid operation when I was sixteen, and he was therefore determined that I must be deaf. However, in spite of repeated whispering from the far end of the room - the most modern testing technique at the time - I disappointed him by always being able to hear what he said.

Boarding school is probably the best possible education for joining any of Her Majesty's establishments, even prison I imagine would not seem much worse. But with a very optimistic outlook on life and little experience I sailed into my lowly appointment where training for future employment was to take place.

I had never used a typewriter before and hated it from the word go, as you were supposed not to look at the letters but do it 'blind', and to prevent one cheating, the letters were covered with a guard; I found it quite impossible. The one key I liked on it was called **MR** which I took to be Mister, but was soon disillusioned when I found out it was Margin Release - whatever that meant. Learning this skill, the criterion of which was to do it at furious and impossible speed, was a purely technical activity and required only concentration and extreme application, at neither of which I excelled. Training to be a Wren also included squad drill; this was certainly a diversion from the typewriter, although no female is designed to march - vital to begin with is knowing left from right. I remember my father telling me about some of our countrymen who were equally incapable of such distinctions and were made to put straw in one boot and hay in the other - the orders were then given as 'hayfoot' - 'strawfoot'; even worse came much later in my career when I had to take a barrack room full of Wrens and drill them, I simply could not get out the order 'ABOUT TURN' at the exact moment when the right foot was correctly poised, and was in danger of forcing the whole squad to climb up the end wall of the building.

The large edifice, (used for our basic training), which we occupied had belonged to London University and was in Camden Hill Road W8, and this we shared with the FANYs (Field Army Nursing Yeomanry) and to whom for some mysterious reason we were forbidden to speak. Thus the first of many rules that I broke was when by great good luck I found a schoolfriend who happened to be among them. Even luckier, this girl had a very powerful motor-bike and frequently we would rush off into the night, me usually riding pillion, and tear round Hyde Park at a furious speed. We always felt better afterwards.

My accommodation was in this vast building, and to find the Mess (where we ate), you had to go through a very long coal hole from which one emerged blinking at the light and ready to eat as fast as possible, so as to finish before anyone else and claim a second helping. We all seemed to be perpetually hungry. There were four girls in my bedroom and one was a very pretty blonde who had been a hairdresser, while the others had equally interesting backgrounds and jobs such as waitresses and dressmakers. Getting to know this jolly medley during our social gatherings was very enlightening. It was here for the first time that I realised the significance of the social divide between dyed-in-the-wool Royal Naval officers (whom we were supposedly trying to emulate), who would wait impatiently for the sun to sink over the yardarm so they could pour their first pink gin with a clear conscience, and those who were expecting a tot of rum - neither of these came our way.

Sharing rooms with all these diverse girls brought to light other discoveries: some were wedded to their vests, which they had been wearing all day, keeping them on even under pyjamas before they tucked down for the night. Putting your bra on outside your vest then of course comes naturally. There was another rather sensitive problem to which some people were more allergic than others, which I had first noticed somewhat earlier, when my mother brought a new nanny into the nursery. My recollection of her white shiny satin blouse with mother of pearl buttons remains to this day associated with what used to be called BO - body odour. I must have been a horrible child, because I immediately pointed out to my mother how she smelled. The vest enthusiasts were rather more prone to this affliction than others, and the first antidote to this misfortune was described euphemistically as a 'deodorant' and was called Odorono; next came 'MUM'. There was an incredible slogan which actually had nothing to do with BO, but warned us that 'Careless Talk Costs Lives'; it was worded 'Be like Dad - Keep Mum'

CARELESS TALK COSTS LIVES

- and used to scream at us in whatever form of advertisement we used to read in those days.

Of course these are superficial observations, and what was far more important and interesting to me was that for the first time, I was mixing on completely equal terms with girls of all classes, whom I would never have had the chance to meet in the ordinary and rather narrow life in which I had been brought up. I very soon found out what made people valuable as colleagues and friends, and that was their integrity. Class had nothing to do with it - I just realised that some people were true to their word and some were not.

Looking back on this broadening of horizons, I also very early discovered that living at such close quarters with complete strangers from every walk of life, the one common denominator which began tentative friendships was a sense of humour; never can this have been more essential. Reflecting on such matters reminds me how harmoniously we all settled down, and how I suspected that my own inadequacies would probably outweigh everybody else's, and that my new comrades would not necessarily agree with me as to what was funny and what was not. Luckily, one of the things we were fighting for was a free country.

Bathrooms in our quarters were few and far between, and one of the battles I fought throughout my Wren career was ensuring my morning bath, getting up earlier and earlier to bag the hot water.

There were a great many rules to obey, and being of a far too independent frame of mind I found myself constantly in trouble. To begin with, we had to be in by nine o'clock at night - one had hardly gone out by that time. We were also expected to exist on ten shillings a week, so there was no way one could hail a taxi home when time was running out. Buses were the cheapest form of transport, but even then I often had to hop off unable to pay the fare.

We were invited to choose a category in which we would like to work; there were not very many at this early stage of the WRNS, so I chose Coder because it sounded mysterious and interesting. I seemed to be frequently up before Miss Buckmaster for misdemeanours of various sorts, who complained that she was very disappointed with my behaviour and punished me by making me scrub floors, which I actually came to prefer to typing or drill. She also demoted me from potential Coder to much inferior Writer. I was now beginning to think that almost anything would be better than this hellhole, and rashly told her of Nancy Osborne's offer of a job at Headquarters, but she quickly disabused me of any likelihood of my being given such a plum position if she had anything to do with it. She added crushingly, 'You are the last person I should recommend for such a prestigious post'. By great good fortune about this time, and shortly after this interchange, I met Nancy Osborne as we squeezed passed each other in the coal hole on our way to lunch, and seized the opportunity of asking her if I might take her up on her kind offer; and before you could say 'knife', there I was at the Wren HQ surrounded by all the old biddies. At least I was safe from Miss Buckmaster.

CHAPTER 2

LONDON AND THE BLITZ

My work was not very demanding and in fact quite interesting as I sifted through endless application forms, all with the two required references and recommendations, (and nobody said anything about typing). Better still, joining the WRNS was quite the most fashionable war work. We had an excellent reputation - earned by the WRNS who had served in the Great War, and quite the most desirable uniform (eventually), although not everyone realised you had to be an officer to get the much admired tricorne hat.

I realised how lucky I had been with my valuable reference. Sometimes I came upon an application form from someone I knew, and was much amused to think how cross my ex-convent English mistress would be if she knew I was in a position of power over her rather obsequious letter trying to sneak in as a Direct Entry Officer. Although the senior Wren officers with whom I worked seemed definitely *personnes de troisième age* as the French politely referred to seniors, they were not without interest.

First, in the office next to mine was Diana Churchill, who looked so exactly like her father, the Prime Minister - very animated and obviously extremely entertaining. Peals of laughter were always attracting our attention, and she would often come through our office and lighten our day. She never did manage to master her tie, and her collar was always adrift with the tie floating in vain for anchorage. With her untidy red hair she was the antithesis of the elegant and exquisitely turned out grey-haired Marchioness of Cholmondeley, who always looked as if she had come straight from the hairdresser, with her swept up coiffure. Unlikely though it may sound, they all got on like a house on fire and were very nice to us juniors.

These officers were by now wearing their uniforms - all obviously couture made in doeskin or the finest serge; the dark navy jackets and skirts had blue stripes at the wrist to denote their rank, and the very desirable tricorne hat with the blue Naval badge in front was the crowning glory. When we lowly Wrens eventually acquired our off the peg issue, the navy suits were made of rough, rather scratchy serge, which if they did not fit, we were allowed to have altered, but only at the Regent Street Branch of the tailor Hector Powe. Daily, at this establishment, Mr Powe was reduced nearly to tears as we tried to make him shorten and tighten these garments, while he fought a losing battle to carry out his quite different strict orders from his Admiralty paymaster.

I always prided myself on being responsible for the smart sailor hats with which Wren ratings were ultimately supplied, because the round melon-shaped hats with stitched brims (which were the first choice) were most unbecoming, and every time I met the Director WRNS, Vera Laughton Mathews - which was frequently as we worked in the same building - she would groan with horror at the angle at which I had perched mine. 'Come here,' she would say, 'I'll put it on properly for you', jamming it down over my ears. This must have strongly influenced her in its demise. The next model was brilliant, based on the sailor's hat but with a beret-like image and with the distinctive ribbon of one's establishment or whatever, very prominent - and this managed to please everyone. The enormous waiting list of applicants wishing to join the WRNS was, in fact, very much dependent on the uniform - smart, dark, navy blue, plain jacket and skirt, whose straight design concealed deficiencies in one's figure, and topped with either the sailor hat or the distinctive tricorne hat - the effect was a winner. The ATS and WAAF were unlucky in that their less attractive khaki and air force blue jackets had wide waist bands which tended to exaggerate the hips - not a popular feature. We were also issued with black ties and white cotton shirts with separate stiff collars and studs; these studs were the bane of our lives and when we first used them, we had to get up half an hour earlier to allow time to master them. Besides all this they gave us unspeakable underwear which included navy blue knickers, 'closed at the knee', known as 'black outs'. We were also supposed to wear thick, black lisle stockings, though these became a myth if you were able to bribe, beg or even steal parachute silk, or later nylon. I will never forget how marvellous the Duchess of Kent looked wearing her Wren officer uniform with her tricorne hat at its most jaunty as she inspected us, The WRNS Guard of Honour, standing outside Drummonds' Bank on her arrival.

We were allowed a meal ticket worth one shilling and threepence for lunch, and I usually went to Lyons Corner House, known as Joey Lyons, in the Strand, where in 1940 one could eat a quite hearty meal for this small sum, which sometimes included a baked apple with chocolate sauce for pudding. This was during what became known as the 'phoney' war. It was a thrill when I discovered that, at the National Gallery, on the opposite side of Trafalgar Square to Drummonds' Bank, I could persuade the authorities to take our meal tickets in exchange for the most mouthwatering sandwiches and a huge cup of coffee, all to be consumed before listening to heavenly lunch-time concerts. These were performed by the finest virtuosi in Europe, many of them having escaped from Nazi Germany, and all who came freely to entertain anyone who cared to listen. We heard Myra Hess, Irene Scharrer, and many other unique performers. I could never forget an enormously fat lady called Oda Schlobodskaya, a renowned performer, who sang a song called *Once I was a tiny blade* (a likely story, I thought, as I giggled irreverently). Upstairs in the National Gallery was an exhibition of paintings by current war artists, which replaced some of the old masters which had been removed to safety from the dangers of London. This was an excellent collection including paintings by Nash, Ravilious, Pitchforth, Eric Gill and many others.

Every day, while crossing Trafalgar Square at lunchtime, we watched the 'dog fights', as they were called, between our brilliant RAF fighters - 'the Few' - in their immortal Spitfires and Hurricanes, and the German bombers escorted by Messerschmitts. Our best day was when the RAF shot down 183 German planes. From then on, the Germans gave up daylight combat and instead took to the Blitz, bombing us Londoners every night. Our billets were Hampstead Way, Broadhurst Gardens, near Finchley Road, quite a half hour journey home every night - so we were sent off early to arrive back before dark. We usually travelled on the number 13 bus, and one evening on our way home, decided to stop and go to the Baker Street cinema. Next morning on our way to work we noticed from the top deck of the bus that the cinema had vanished - completely taken out by a bomb; it must have just missed us by inches. Sometimes the 13 bus made history by going through Hyde Park when the normal route was blocked by fire engines or road damage.

Searching for signs of life

It is also amazing to think that in spite of this nightly disruption caused by the bombardment, there was always a copy of *The Times* to buy on my way to work. How on earth did they do it?

On another memorable night a stick of bombs came down on Broadhurst Gardens, and every other house on the opposite side of the road to us was flattened. These were formally quite decent Edwardian terraced houses which had the use of the communal garden behind. When the Blitz began we were no longer allowed to sleep in our bedrooms upstairs, but had to shelter in the semi basement; this gave access to the garden by going up a small flight of steps and through some French windows. We slept in double bunks much too close to each other, and the snoring was horrific - some of us spent fruitless hours arming ourselves with slippers and hurling them at the worst offenders. The night the stick of bombs fell, our French windows were blown open violently by the blast and clouds of evil explosive smelling smoke rushed in. In the morning when I went up to the top floor to have my bath as usual, the stairs felt very shaky, and over the road firemen were searching for any signs of life. Typically, Vera Laughton Mathews came round immediately to visit us and see the damage, and find out how we had coped.

In spite of the Blitz, I still went to the theatre as often as I could afford; there were marvellous shows on: Noel Coward's *Blythe Spirit* with Margaret Rutherford as Madame Arcati; Joyce Grenfell enjoying instant stardom in successive reviews and also the Proms at Queen's

Hall - until that, too, was bombed. I don't ever remember a show being stopped for a raid while I was in a theatre, although the audience often winced at some rather too near explosions. The ack-ack g u n s were tireless, and with barrage balloons which were strategically placed, forced the planes as high as possible, plus giving us a lot of comfort. You could distinguish between the German engine noises and our own, droning loudly in the background, accompanied by the violent ack-ack gunfire - I can hear them now. I also remember having to rush teeth cleaning, as the sound of brushing in one's head muffled the warning shriek of a bomb.

Safer by tube

The vast majority of Londoners would take their overnight requirements and decamp to the Underground, where the platforms we re jammed with bunk beds and people sleeping on anything available. However, lots of parties still went on, complete with howling children and a great deal of community singing. In fact, if you were trying to catch a train, it was quite a job to squeeze past to get aboard. I much preferred travelling by bus, but during the Blitz it definitely felt safer to go home at night by tube.

Occasionally I went to visit a great aunt in Kensington, one of my grandmother's sisters called Christian Beaton, after whom I was named, although we called her Aunt Tin. She was Cecil Beaton's stepmother, a great character, and always wore rather loose, long dresses, very often with fur and/or beads round the hem, and very large hats with lots of feathers. She was usually accompanied by a badtempered, spoiled Peke, who was inclined to bite. She had so many nephews and nieces, great-nephews and great-nieces who all sent her presents for Christmas, that she decided the best course of action was never to unwrap any of them and then send them all back the next Christmas quite randomly. The result was that you never sent her anything unworthy, as there was a very good chance you would get it back. Aunt Tin lived in a rather stuffy hotel in great comfort in Kensington, and would always insist on my staying to dinner and regaling her and her friends with my latest triumphs and disasters. I also recall she greatly admired my trousers, which were quite daring apparel in those far off days.

Every so often I would have a long weekend and catch the sleeper train on Friday night from King's Cross to Speanbridge (in Inverness-shire) to stay with my grandmother. The train was always full, no hope of a sleeper even if I could have afforded it. One sat in the corridor on one's luggage, sustained by the promise of two wonderful nights in a proper bed with linen sheets. On one visit I had to change at Glasgow, and not only change trains but stations. People were always friendly and helpful in this sort of predicament and I was given a lift in an enormous bakery van, the driver of which insisted on seeing me into my next train and treating me to a rug.

My grandmother was a passionate gardener and indoctrinated me into some of her horticultural secrets. Blarour, Speanbridge, was her one-time famous and hospitable house and garden, which nestled neatly into a narrow niche in the purple heather covered braes of Lochaber. Sweeping out in front was a vast lawn with a variety of well-established rhododendron bushes either side; this was mown once a week by a horsedrawn mower, very laboursaving as the cutter was hugely wide. The horse must have been a cart horse, with its feathery fetlocks and large stride, and left a pleasant, lingering smell of grass and horse in its wake. Beyond the lawn the land dropped steeply away, with the curve of the drive encircling it, and the view from the house of the distant range of rolling hills was visible across the Glen in which the River Spean flowed. All this produced the tonic required to brace oneself for the return to harsh reality of 'doing one's bit'.

During these visits, I persuaded her to tell me about her early days when she was one of seven sisters and two brothers living in a large rambling old house near Perth. Her mother had died when they were all quite young, and her father, known as YF (your father), made them have lessons for six months of the year at home, while for the other six months he took them travelling all over Europe. My grandmother fell in love with a doctor, Frederick Berry, who hailed from Alnwick in Northumberland and who was a member of the Indian Civil Service; when she was eighteen she sailed out to Bombay (suitably chaperoned) and married him. She then went with him to his remote station in south India where she lived completely cut off from any other Europeans. One day he came home to tell her that he must isolate himself from her as he had been in contact with cholera, and not long after this he contracted the disease and died. My grandmother, expecting a baby (my mother), at this point had to produce her baby with the help of her Indian Ayah, and travelled back to Bombay and eventually Scotland. Here, she resumed her family life near Perth with her rather delicate baby who was doted upon by an eager bunch of aunts and uncles. In less than a year she had become a bride, a widow and a mother and was still barely twenty.

Arriving at King's Cross in the early morning after one of these weekends, when it should have been pitch black, I found the whole sky lit up as if in brilliant daylight. Only it wasn't daylight. The docks and the whole east end of London were ablaze. We became very used to the bombing every night in London, but having been away for a couple of nights one noticed it more.

My father had joined HMS *Britannia* aged 12, the Royal Naval Officers' training ship of his day (about 1905) and served throughout WW1. His most memorable experience I guess was when at Gallipoli he was sunk three times in one day without getting his feet wet. Now retired, he was responsible for the Port of London Authority where the large glazed Rotunda had to be somehow protected from bombs. I rang him up from time to time: 'How are you getting on Pa? Does anyone look after you?' In spite of never having even boiled a kettle, and after a lifetime of naval servants pandering to his every whim, he seemed content. 'I have learned how to cook' he said. 'But what do you cook ?' I enquired. 'I cook water and get out of bed very carefully to save making my bed'. Sailors are extremely adaptable.

CHAPTER 3

⚓

VERA LAUGHTON MATHEWS
Director of WRNS

In 1938 Vera Laughton Mathews was appointed Director of the WRNS by the Admiralty, and her first task was to have a recruitment drive, as it was obvious that many of the shore jobs of the Royal Navy could be done by girls. She was the ideal person to set it all up being of a Royal Naval family herself; her job began immediately, and as the replies to her advertisements streamed in, she worked all day and much of the night.

She found herself dealing with many marvellously helpful Admirals as well as a curmudgeonly minded faction, who were of the 'Women in the Senior Service ? Over my dead body!' frame of mind. But with her charm and determination she usually got her way, although she had a real problem getting the officers' ration of stripes sorted out. Apparently, most Royal Navy senior officers are very stripe minded and refuse to communicate with anyone sporting too few. As the Admiralty had not thought it necessary to allow Wrens more than three blue stripes, however senior, there were times therefore when impasse ensued. Eventually she persuaded their Lordships that Superintendent WRNS, of which there were only five at the time, must be allowed to wear four blue stripes, and that she, the Director, should be permitted one broad and one narrow, equivalent to a Rear Admiral. With no staff to begin with and minimal organisation, Wrens were interviewed and either immediately taken on or not. There was no hanging about, and with no training and no uniform as yet, they often fell headfirst into their new jobs.

Vera Laughton Mathews was a remarkable woman. Deeply Christian, she knew exactly what sort of WRNS she wanted from the start, and fought all the regiments of bureaucrats and civil servants singlehandedly to get it right. A dedicated, hands-on person, she did everything herself, interviewing and choosing her closest staff officers and making all the important decisions quite independently. These colleagues all became great friends and stuck with her through thick and thin until the war was over, when she wrote much the best book about her Service, called *Blue Tapestry*. Her success must be measured by remarks made in Parliament during a debate when the Civil Lord of the Admiralty stated that 'the WRNS had become a real, living integral part of the Royal Navy, and all that that implies, with its centuries of great tradition and high performance....I have no doubt that if you gave the WRNS half a chance they would be perfectly prepared to sail a battleship.'

To begin with, the categories you could serve in were very limited; you could only be a Writer (office worker), Coder, Cook, Steward, Driver or Despatch Rider, but it was soon discovered how adaptable and eager all the girls were, and requests for Wrens in many other departments came from every direction. For example, some were employed as Minewatchers, stationed in lookout pill boxes along the Thames and other vantage points, whose job it was to take the bearings of any mines dropped into the water during air raids, which had to be retrieved as soon as possible; Torpedo Wrens were trained on the spot in the care and maintenance of torpedoes and depth charges, looking after all the delicate mechanisms. Wrens were also asked to do secret work at Bletchley Park, and were much cheered by a message from Winston Churchill which said 'glad to hear the Wrens are laying so well without clucking' - reference to their ability to keep their work secret. Most popular category of all was Boating Wren - they were allowed to wear bell-bottoms and a very smart white lanyard (a cord worn round the neck to hold a whistle or knife) when uniform at last became available. More about all these later on.

It is not perhaps generally known that several hundred Wrens were killed due to enemy action during the war, some torpedoed on their way to appointments abroad, and others bombed in their Wreneries.

Wren Freda Bonner was nearly one of these casualties and tells of her experience sailing from South Africa in the *Empress of Canada*, a liner turned trooper of 21,516 tons, which had sailed from Durban

1st March 1943 with 1800 troops on board, including 400 Italian prisoners of war. On 13th/14th March she was torpedoed twice by the Italian submarine *Leonardo da Vinci*, 400 miles south of Las Palmas, and sank within 20 minutes with a loss of 392 lives, among them 44 of the crew.

'Shortly after 11pm we heard a dull thud, far, far below us - and we knew at once that we had been torpedoed. A few minutes later the ship stopped dead. No alarm sounded, there were no lights; and even the emergency system failed. A brilliant or freak shot had hit us

RMS Empress of Canada

amidships in the engine room. At first there was an uncanny silence and then we heard urgent footsteps on the stairs. We Wrens were all together in one cabin and in a few minutes we had put on our coats and lifejackets....when we found our boat station, our boat was overturned in the water, the ship had heeled over....the decks were at a sharp angle, half the lifeboats could not be launched or had over-turned....Naval officers took charge throwing rafts and floats into the sea, letting down ropes, getting off refugees and the Italian prisoners of war who jumped into the sea.

The Italian submarine Captain observed the Geneva Convention ruling to allow time for the passengers and crew to abandon ship - then torpedoed her again. As we were all pushing away from the ship, suddenly in front of us the seas opened and a huge black monster came up from the deep, it was the submarine. At gunpoint its Captain ordered the nearest lifeboat to come alongside, from which he took the only Italian officer.

It was about two hours later that the *Canada* suddenly upended and with a dreadful, awful, roaring noise plunged down into the depth of the sea. This dreadful, awful roar remained with me night after night for nearly a year. It was a long night...there were many cries for help....at long last the dawn came. All around us were rafts, boats with red sails and Carley floats and still many people in the sea, their lifebelts having supported them all through the night....there were also the fins of sharks and barracudas. On the second afternoon a Sunderland flying boat flew over us, we knew then that rescue was on the way. On the fourth evening as the sun was setting we saw HMS *Boreas*. We watched her stopping over and over again to pick up survivors and soon it was our turn. Every stop the Captain made endangered his ship....two days later we were landed at Freetown....it was a sad accounting, although all six Wrens and the ten women refugees had been saved the cost had been high. Over 200 had been lost; these losses would have been much higher if it had not been for the Royal Naval Officers who gave their lives 'doing their duty.'

On the last lap of her long journey home to Dublin, Freda was told to change trains for the fourth time, and exhausted, she said 'Must I change yet again?' A woman beside her said 'You're lucky to be travelling - don't you know there's a war on?'

CHAPTER 4

DEGAUSSING AND MINES

M y escape from London came at last, after about a year, when I was promoted Leading Wren: I proudly wore the badge with the blue anchor on my left upper arm, my 'hook', as it was known.

Put in charge of a small unit of about twelve Wrens, my job was to run the degaussing range based at Coalhouse Fort near East Tilbury on the Thames; it was from this Fort that the illustrious Queen Elizabeth I was supposed to have harangued her troops saying: 'I know I have the body of a weak and feeble woman, but I have the heart and stomach of a King and a King of England too'. Stirring stuff. Even during the fourteenth and fifteenth centuries there had been temporary structures built to guard the ferry at the important Thames River crossing from Tilbury to Gravesend, but Henry VIII had more ambitious defences in mind when he ordered five block-houses to be constructed, designed for artillery. These were sited at West and East Tilbury (this was Coalhouse Fort) on the Essex bank and also at Gravesend, Milton and Higham on the Kentish side, to prevent enemy shipping from advancing up the Thames, and built D-shaped with the rounded side facing the river.

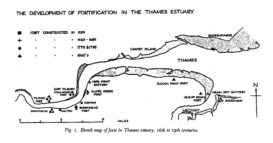

THE DEVELOPMENT OF FORTIFICATION IN THE THAMES ESTUARY

Fig. 1. Sketch map of forts in Thames estuary, 16th to 19th centuries.

Later forts were built on these and other sites, but what was left of Coalhouse Fort disappeared beneath a Victorian coastal defence fort, set in parkland beside the river and completed in 1874. This was later modified to take modern armament and is considered one of the finest examples of an armoured casemated fort in the UK.

Coalhouse Fort

The Degaussing Control Tower was a brick structure between two gun houses with a concrete roof. It was surrounded by the ramparts which were used for visual signalling by our Sea Scouts to ships, and to the Cliffe Fort on the other side of the river.

My appointment was to be Degaussing Recorder in Charge, and the job consisted of setting up and organising a degaussing range across the Thames. The Oxford Dictionary describes 'degaussing' quite succinctly: it is to 'neutralize the magnetic field of a ship by encircling with a conductor carrying electric currents', thus enabling the ship to sail safely over a magnetic mine.

The unit of magnetic flux density is named after Karl Gauss, who was a German

A magnetic mine

mathematician of the 18th century. Luckily I was not expected to do anything technical, but I would have to control all the processes of instrumentation for the ships on the range. Totally dependent as Britain was on her imports, it was a disaster that we were losing so many valuable merchant ships, not only to submarines in the Atlantic but to these new magnetic mines. As every ship was full of essential requirements for the war effort, it was urgently necessary to set up a system for their safety. Later, all Royal Navy ships had such magnetic neutralizing protection built in, but all other ships had to have their vulnerability tested over these ranges, and the prescribed wire coils carrying the correct amount of electric current had to be fitted right round the hull. These magnetic mines were designed and suitable only for laying in narrow and shallow waters. All of our Naval ports where such conditions prevailed were set up with degaussing ranges; German U-boats and planes were known to have laid these mines in such ports and there were many in the shallows of the Thames estuary, often dropped by parachute. Ships had to have their magnetic signatures checked both on the way in and out of any entrance, as any change of cargo would alter the magnetic emission. On reaching the danger zone, the Pilot would bring the Degaussing Officer out to the ship in his boat, the measurements would be taken and the result communicated to the scientist in our office by Sea Scouts, part of our contingent, using semaphore or morse code. He would then prescribe the correct electric current for the coils. My job was to direct operations, including ordering ships over the range, and to record, file and distribute the information to the people concerned - so I did feel very proud to be in close contact with the safety of our fellow sailors.

Although I had no training for anything except the abortive typing and a little squad drill, I was expected, aged about twenty, to be responsible not only for the efficiency and smooth running of the range and the office but also for the welfare of my Wrens. This was no sinecure. It is hardly possible to believe nowadays how breath -takingly ignorant girls of that era were. It was years before the Pill, mothers usually ducked out of the embarrassing duty of telling daughters the Facts of Life; parents were very detached in those days and apart from the perfunctory peck on greeting, I do not remember ever having such a thing as a hug. I had a school friend at my convent whose mother had actually told her what went on, but it was impossible to imagine our parents behaving like that, so we thought it frightfully funny and refused to believe it. We were brought up that 'Nice Girls Didn't'- so we pretended to know it all, but all we really knew was that somehow if they 'Did', they might subsequently produce a baby and this was the worst disgrace and disaster that could possibly occur. (This abysmal state of artlessness is exemplified by Mary Hilton Jones in her story which appears later, on page 99).

Now that we were all at Coalhouse Fort, we were surrounded by a wonderful array of young men, soldiers manning the Fort, sailors and marines of all ranks - and we were the only girls in sight. There was only the local pub to sustain this potential social life so we started by drinking in the public bar with the sailors, and then progressed on to the Saloon Bar with the officers. Although we were all longing to fall in love and very susceptible to flattery of any kind, I am glad to say that even with all this choice and constant changes in personnel, none of us started any very serious love affairs; but there were anxious times when a girl, having indulged in a very enthusiastic smoochy French kiss - this it was rumoured could cause babies - would feel obliged to take drastic measures. There were a number of these recommended, such as taking frequent very hot baths while drinking strong gin and quinine, violently jumping up and down or even falling down stairs. Luckily no disastrous results occurred.

At East Tilbury I and my degaussing Wrens were billeted in an old cold vicarage minus the vicar; sleeping four to a room in camp beds with only linoleum on the floor. We were always cold and one girl had frightful asthma so I often had to sit up with her through the night. She was terrified of reporting sick in case she was made to leave. The caretaker and his wife, Mr and Mrs Entwhistle, were rather under-paid, judging by the inadequate way we were fed; he was a most ill favoured, grumpy and grumbling character and seemed to resent such a noisy and cheerful invasion of his household, while she was a poor little doormat and whenever possible we took her side. We used to go out before breakfast and pick mushrooms to supplement her husband's offerings; (goodness knows what else we ate but there was never enough) and my memories of the other food seem to blur between sardines and raspberry jam, somehow on the same plate -

and a first breakfast consisting of porridge. When Ruth Ashton, a great friend to this day, complained that she did not like porridge, Mr Entwhistle was furious with her, denied that it was porridge and claimed it was kedgeree. I rest my case.

Ruth was very attractive with a wonderful mop of red hair, and was always much in demand with our office mates, Peter, Jerry et al, who looked upon us with a slightly proprietary air during our evening entertainment in the public bar with them. They also queued up to ask Ruth's help when they discovered she was a willing dab hand at the sewing machine. It is well known that sailors are very vain, and are well aware of how becoming is their square rig sailor's uniform. They would keep a best (or tiddley) suit for high days and holidays; this had to be skin tight, hardly allowing for sitting down but with the bell-bottoms suitably flared out to swing in a provocative manner. Ruth could always be relied on to produce the desired effect. She was also very adventurous, and one day she bought a car for £11 from one of the sea-scouts, soon discovering how to drive it with very inexpert help from me, after which we went all over the place in it. Sadly one day it died, so she left it in the Albert Dock and forgot about it until about five years later. By this time married to Jimmy Joly, also in the Navy, she told him where it was. Naturally they rushed back to see if it was still there - and it was - so Jimmy did all sorts of things to it, cleaned it up and sold it for £40! No bad deal in those days.

Perhaps Mr Entwhistle had reason to be cross, because as well as putting up with us he suffered from thyroid trouble and had a rather obvious goitre. In our flippant and heartless manner and after yet another ghastly meal we often used to say 'I do hope one day someone will come and take him away and cut his throat.' Imagine my shock horror when on my twenty first birthday somebody did exactly that, and my birthday treat was an invitation to view the poor man's remains in his coffin, returned to his home after the fatal operation and where his lying in state took place on the dining room table. I remember trying tactfully to duck out of this by saying, 'No, really, I would rather think of him as he was'. The day had begun rather dramatically at work, when I was called to the telephone by the hospital, and asked to tell Mrs Entwhistle that her husband had died during the operation and would I please inform her. There was of course no telephone at the vicarage. I remember putting on my uniform hat, which somehow seemed necessary for the sombre occasion, and walking up to the vicarage; I then persuaded her to sit down in her kitchen where I broke the dread news, which to my relief did not seem to displease her.

This however was still my twenty first birthday. By the time the sun was over the yardarm, several cheerful friends, Philip, Peter and Jerry, and our degaussing sailors, rolled up with bottles of this and that and before long we had this party going. Unfortunately it was a rather small room for such a party, and apart from the macabrely occupied dining room table, there was nowhere much to put things. Mrs E was just having her third gin and getting rather tearful, when Jerry, after raising his glass and proposing a toast to 'Up spirits!', became intoxicated by his own wit, howled with laughter, and absentmindedly put his glass down on the coffin. This caused the whole party to disintegrate into uncontrollable giggles, whereupon Mrs E, overcome with such a heady mixture of emotions and no longer able to assimilate what was going on, sank silently to the floor. Thus I have never been able to forget my coming of age.

CHAPTER 5

⚓

HOW TO TELL WHAT'S WHAT
IN THE ROYAL NAVY

Nancy Spain, who had been a freelance journalist before the war, joined up as a Wren Motor Transport Driver and wrote a contemporary book about her experiences in the WRNS called *Thank You - Nelson*. She gives a very good description of the Proper or 'pusser' Navy, which she soon learned to identify, and I much appreciated her distinction when seeing any young officer with straight gold rings on his sleeves, denoting Royal Navy. This was always a matter of pride, although one began to admire the RNVR, Royal Naval Volunteer Reserve or 'Wavy Navy', (zigzag gold stripes at the wrist to denote rank) and the RNR, Royal Naval Reserve (plaited gold stripes) equally as the war developed.

Saluting was a sure way of telling if someone was Proper Navy - it was a very individual movement. My father had the most distinguished salute I have ever seen. He somehow managed to make it look totally dashing, but also instinctive. The precise action is not easy to describe, but complete flatness of the wrist joint is essential with just a little tilt towards the eyebrow, the whole carried out with a very *dégagé* air.

Spain's book is an amusing racy read with a great deal of imagined conversation, with which she manages to convey certain typical rather piratical characters, usually Chief Petty Officers or other old salts. Wren Storekeepers for instance, had to be taught by these experienced and knowledgeable characters in the traditional but endlessly complicated method of issuing stores. It seems there was no very logical way of guessing that, for example, spark plugs, paint-brushes, knives and forks or anything that could wear out were supplied under the soubriquet of 'consumable', or that telescopes, spanners, compasses, and semaphoring apparatus would be described as 'permanent stores', and that the issuing of all these involved endless signatures and authorising and were then on 'Permanent Loan'. If these essential items became damaged or stolen, the Commanding Officer would have to produce a quantity of documents before a replacement was reissued, and if these were unforthcoming he would have to pay for the items himself. One of her favourite Chiefs had been a stoker (engineer), and to complicate his life further he favoured age-old railway company procedure for animals travelling by rail. 'Well Sir, I don't rightly know what to charge 'ee for your tortoise. Cats is cats, and dogs is dogs, but by company rules tortoises is hinsects'. Quite irrelevant but it seemed that the Navy had not changed much in its storekeeping or accounting methods since Pepys' day and continued to operate in its own arcane ways.

Relevant to my degaussing range are Nancy Spain's several experiences as a Wren Motor Driver when she became rather too closely involved with magnetic mines. These were often randomly dropped in the most inconvenient places, and somehow had to be made safe and disposed of. She was driving the Mine Disposal Officer one day (when his lorry had broken down) in order to remove a mine which had been dropped on the rocks with its parachute on the undercliff walk, at a point where the sea would have covered it at high tide. The mine was about seven feet high, shaped like a large cigar and weighing about eight hundred pounds, forcing all the residential houses on the front to be evacuated. The Mine Disposal Officer said cheerfully that the mine would kill anything standing upright within five hundred yards. There was a steam crane on the site so they set to work, and the crane driver produced 'a little cage of ropes and bars' which the MDO attached to the mine. Then the straining from all angles began, backing and advancing the crane, lowering the arm with much shouting and waving. After a good hour, a huge sucking noise announced the mine's release and it swung high in the air with 'little bits of seaweed, crabs and other crustacea dripping from it'. It was then lowered reverently beside the lorry, and the MDO casually whispered to Nancy that he had been unable to take the 'sting' out of it because of the rust. Somehow the three of them pushed eight hundred pounds of steel and high explosive up two shaky railway sleepers and on to a steel girder into the lorry. Nancy says, 'I climbed up beside the mine with a rope and made it a little collar at each end to hold it down and lashed these round the pillar of the van. The springs sagged delightfully'. The MDO presented her with the silk cord of the parachute, which she proudly wore as a dressing gown sash.

Another time Spain had to assist when they managed to extract a magnetic mine which had become lodged under the bandstand at a pleasure resort, 'a great big thing with horrid little horns sticking out all over it'. This time they had dragooned some soldiers in to help, and with superhuman efforts pushing and shoving, finally lifted the unwieldy load into a tipping truck on its way to Nancy's lorry. Unfortunately they forgot it was a tipping truck and failed to do up the catch. As it tipped, the mine rolled ponderously down the hill accelerating as it went. This time, although it was supposed to have been made safe, Nancy says, 'I have never seen a seashore so quickly deserted - I found myself under the bandstand with my mouth full of sand.'

CHAPTER 6

⚓

ABOUT TURN, GIRLS

Returning to my earlier observations about females not being designed to drill, it is fascinating to hear what Audrey Johnson has to say on the subject in her book called *Do March in Step Girls*.

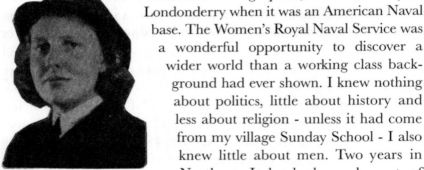

Audrey Johnson in original model hat.

'This is a Wren's account of almost four years as a Wireless Telegraphist, and set mostly in Londonderry when it was an American Naval base. The Women's Royal Naval Service was a wonderful opportunity to discover a wider world than a working class background had ever shown. I knew nothing about politics, little about history and less about religion - unless it had come from my village Sunday School - I also knew little about men. Two years in Northern Ireland changed most of that.

We were extremely patriotic, ready to give our lives rather than allow that man Hitler to tell us how to live, and so proud to be part of Britain's Royal Navy. It was a wild time in Derry. There were endless invitations to dinners on board escort ships, dancing, blind dates, more dancing. More than half of Derry hated our guts, and there were Germans in Southern Ireland just a few miles down the road. And all this time the war went on. Escort ships from Western Approaches battled across the North Atlantic, many of them never to return, while U-boats refuelled off the coast of Donegal. It was a desperate world out there.

Convoys to and from America were keeping this country going, and although we danced and flirted we took our part in the Battle of the Atlantic very seriously.'

Audrey continues: 'Now, girls! Let's see if we can all manage to halt at the same time, shall we? Ready?…By the left, quick march. Left, right, left, right, squad….halt! At ease.'

I was not at ease, I had never been so cold in my life. The east wind sent knives around my ears, my nose dripped, chilblains were killing me and we were off again. 'By the left, quick march, left, right, left, right….' We must have looked a ragged bunch of young women, still in civvies - from smart to dowdy - faces pinched, noses red and few of us able to distinguish left from right. A few people had stopped to watch, but not for long.

'Oh, do march in step girls!' the voice was pleading. 'It looks so much nicer.' She was a lovely petty officer , who knew so well how to deal with newly recruited Wrens during their first few days in the service - nothing like the squad drill I had seen on newsreels, with red faced sergeants bawling their heads off. Our petty officer looked up at the sky and said, 'I think that will do for today, girls, looks as if it will snow before long. Left, right, left, right, squad….halt!', and we were fractionally better that time. 'Right, about….turn!' But we were not to be allowed to get away with that muddle of indecision, whether snow was threatening or not. 'As you were'. And we shuffled round again. 'Now, think about it, make sure which is your right and we will try again.' Nothing had ever been as cold as this. Tears trailed down my frozen face and I longed to blow my nose. My poor feet were agony. 'Right then? All ready? Know which is your right? Right about….turn.' And only two got it wrong that time, before we marched, hands clenched, thumbs facing forward, arms swinging, legs moving more or less in time towards our new Wren quarters. We would be free till supper.

Audrey also makes interesting social observations: 'Oh, hullo! I was told you were coming'. Impeccable, well-to-do accents rang through the building. 'Marjorie was at school with you, I understand; and I believe you know the Somebody-hyphen-Somebodies.' 'Oh, you're Rosemary. Daddy told me to keep a lookout for you. He's at the Admiralty with your uncle.' Everybody seemed to know somebody of importance. 'Oh, hello! You're Primrose aren't you? Thought you must be. Ann told me to look out for you. She was at school with your sister'. And two more new recruits sat down to chat. I knew no-one. There was no-one to know the stepdaughter of a foreman engineer from Leicester.

My mother had not wanted me to join the Land Army, because it would ruin my hands, neither had she wanted me to go into a munitions factory because she did not think I would like the type of woman there. I listened to the assured voices round me. This was as bad the other way round. I had no-one to talk about. I knew nothing. I'd been nowhere. I felt unsure, lonely and out of place and could not work out how I had been accepted for this service, that appeared to choose its entrants with such care. I had nothing they asked for, certainly no educational qualifications. I had a feeling I must be the only girl who had left school at fourteen. But I was not going to mention that to anyone, and night school elocution lessons had helped a bit.

I had been strolling round our village at home with Joyce who had a boyfriend in the RAF. 'Wouldn't mind joining the WAAF', she said. I replied 'If I joined anything it would be the WRNS. It's the most difficult service to get into', I observed, but some weeks later we both applied to join. If we were turned down for the Senior Service we could still apply for the WAAF, and if that failed there was always the ATS. But in spite of the odds, we were eventually both accepted. I was thrilled at the prospect of the smart navy blue suit, white shirt and collar and black stockings and of course the hat. I never could stand the khaki stockings of the ATS, and the Air Force blue ones weren't much better.

Our first few days were spent trying to get the squad drill into some form of agreement between its members, something that from the very first day never failed to amuse me in a ridiculous way. The moment the command came, 'Right girls….shortest on the right, tallest on the left….in three ranks….fall in!' I found it funny. Each morning after our first few days we would form into a squad outside the quarters, still in our civvies, to march about half a mile through the centre of town to the wireless college, marching back for lunch and then marching to college again for the afternoon session. My chilblains were my worst problem, and one morning as I struggled to keep up with the endless left, right, left right, at a quick march, my stiff hurting feet in their stiff, cold unyielding sensible shoes, I slipped in the hard-packed, slippery snow and sat down in the middle of the main road, rush hour traffic; the back half of the squad cannoned into one another and the front half marched on oblivious, like a worm cut in two by a spade. I simply could not get up. I could not even begin to try. The petty officer stood over me, making sure I wasn't hurt, then pleading with me to 'please get up' so that the traffic could continue on its way and the Wrens could get to the college. But it was impossible. Painful chilblains completely forgotten, I just sat there completely helpless with laughter.

Falling over was funny enough, when I was part of the Senior Service and supposed to be taken seriously by the public in my war winning business. But the ridiculous sight of the separate happenings in the two sections of the squad were better than anything I had ever seen at the pictures. I just sat on the ground, watching the unaware front section making its neat way forward, the rest of us incapable of anything but uncontrollable giggles.'

To me, this is the most relevant chapter of her book and so I will just leave Audrey there, in the middle of the road!

CHAPTER 7

——— ⚓ ———

LESSONS IN BECOMING AN OFFICER
AND A LADY

Having survived a longish spell degaussing, I was recommended to go before the Officers Selection Board for a possible commission. To my surprise I was accepted, and sent to Greenwich where the Officer Training Course took place. Nothing could have been a greater contrast in our living conditions than the squalid vicarage at East Tilbury and the white Palladian colonnades and domes of Greenwich Palace. Sailing down the river by ferry to arrive by boat and disembark at the pier - a familiar landing place for people of such renown as Henry Vlll, Elizabeth l, Drake, Raleigh, Queen Anne and Pepys - was a landmark in my career. In fact, this inspired choice of background to begin the Officers Training Course could not have impressed us more. Although I had known about Christopher Wren and his splendid churches all over London, to actually inhabit one of his buildings was an amazing experience, and as I have always loved big rivers, it was a joy still to be beside this famous and historic waterway. The Thames was redolent with antiquity, alive with the ships and boats that were constantly moving up and down, accompanied by those beautiful river barges with their magnificent red rig proceeding leisurely on their way, weaving unconcerned through the busy river traffic where steam gives way to sail, with fog horns and hooting adding to the bustling atmosphere.

Here one was to learn not only how to become an Officer but hopefully a 'lady' too. There were other things you apparently needed to know, besides not to eat peas off one's knife. The lectures we listened to varied from the utterly boring to brilliant, with one on Navigation and Admiralty Procedure in the latter category. Admiral

Sir William Goodenough did not so much seem to lecture as simply tell us things we might find useful in the Navy, the Proper Navy of course, and in such a way that he seemed to have only just begun when he was saying 'Thank you'. The Ministry of Economic Warfare sent a representative, the Deputy Judge Advocate, and the NAAFI (Navy, Army & Air Force Institute) also came to tell us what we needed to know, and some senior Wren Officers additionally enlightened us. This intelligence was all somewhat blighted by the extreme cold, the difficulties of ever finding one's way through the labyrinth of unidentifiable stone corridors to where you ought to be, and how to get there on time, (which in the Navy always meant five minutes beforehand). The difficulties of ever finding a bath in this elegant edifice, or the way back to one's cabin, and clad in the flimsiest of dressing gowns, also remain very strong impressions.

Although the bombing went on, Christopher Wren's capacious vaults, known as the catacombs, provided perfect safety, even if in imperfect comfort, perhaps in a hammock or lying like a fish on a fishmonger's slab in a treble bunk. Thankfully it was quite beyond the power of Hitler, at this stage of the war, to make much impression on this solidly stone built monument.

But what a thrill it was to find yourself in the Painted Hall, and for breakfast at that, with Thornhill's early 18th century paintings, wonderfully and dramatically lit by hundreds of shaded candles in silver candlesticks and illuminated by indirect flood-lighting. We had all our meals in this unforgettable Hall, which engendered a quiet polite atmosphere and murmured conversation. Wren Stewards waited on us; we had beautiful white linen napkins; the delicious coffee was hot and there was plenty of it - served in large white china cups emblazoned with the blue Admiralty stamp.

After two weeks of this exalted treatment I was appointed to the Cypher course, but by this time I had discovered that coding and cyphering were in fact extremely tedious, and apart from occasionally interpreting an exciting signal there was nothing much to it. I felt rather like Mr Toad in *Wind in the Willows* when I changed 'enthusiasms' again and decided that Plotting was a much more interesting career. As a Plotter you would be entitled to read all those laboriously decoded messages anyway, and also have complete access to secret documents, such as the Pink List, which was specially valuable as it listed the whereabouts of all the ships in the Navy. You could thus discover where your latest young man was likely to be. However I was doomed to go through the Cypher course, and after another two weeks at Greenwich, was contemplating a gloomy future when I was electrified by suddenly receiving a signal which ordered me to report to Plymouth as Plotting Officer. I seemed to be hoist with my own petard.

Before we leave Greenwich, Mary Wynn Jones wants to tell us of how she became one of those elegant expert Wren Stewards appointed to the Naval Officers' Mess in the famous Painted Hall of the College, renowned for the good service of its Wren staff.

Having good sailor's blood in her veins (going back to her great grandfather), and working as a nanny in London until October 1940, Mary decided to sign up there and then on the spur of the moment. Not fancying being a Cook, she volunteered as a Cabin-Steward: 'Almost before the ink was dry on my application form I was given my Medical and was passed as 'in good condition and fit for duty'. 'My call up papers swiftly followed and having satisfied myself that my employer had a suitable nanny replacement, I duly reported to the Royal Naval College, Greenwich on 16th December 1940. Here I went through a brief introductory course on what was expected of me as a member of the Senior Service, after which I took the Oath of Allegiance to my King and country and to the WRNS in particular. I was then issued with my pay book - two shillings (10p) per day - given my Service Number 9266, sent to the Quartermaster to collect my uniform, and was pitched headlong into the strange exciting life of becoming a Wren.

By stages I survived the back-breaking task of swabbing the dusty flag-stoned floors of the lower regions of the College with a long-handled mop at the crack of cold, dark dawns, graduated to the pleasanter tasks of bed-making for the junior officers, where my nanny training stood me in good stead, and thus to the cleaning of 'cabins'. No luxury of vacuum cleaner, nor even the more modest carpet sweeper in this austere establishment - instead I learned to clean carpets by the almost archaic method of first sprinkling them liberally with wet tea leaves, which were then brushed up plus the dust so collected by them by vigorous use of a hard-bristled broom, the smaller mats being taken 'below' to be either shaken or beaten depending on their size, outside. Then it was down on hands and knees to apply wax polish to the wood or lino surrounds, ditto to buff to a shine, except where there was sufficient floor space to be able to tie dusters to the feet and slide energetically over the surface - most effective and great fun, especially swishing and swooshing down the long corridors. Turn and turn about, I and my colleagues had the unenviable task of scrubbing the wide cold stone stairs leading from one floor to another....all of which provided excellent exercise, though there was not a great deal of fun to be had from having afterwards to wash out wax polish-impregnated dusters and rough floorcloths with nothing more than hard yellow soap and hot water in horridly chilly, ancient stone sinks.'

Quite a contrast follows. 'Finally I was introduced via the Wren Officers Mess in the Queen Anne Block of the College, presided over by the oh-so-elegant and delightful Miss French (Superintendent WRNS in charge) to the niceties of waiting at table. 'Menu and food from the left, drinks from the right, anticipate needs' was her mantra. 'I learned quickly, seeming to have a natural instinct for it, with the advantage of coming from a good middle class home with properly set table, and parents who taught their children to respect it. Here I was happy to stay, once I had recovered from the sheer terror of my first day, when neat in my Mess uniform of princess line white coat, its blue mandarin collar opening over knotted black tie under fresh white shirt collar, and with pristine white gloves to protect my hands from hot plates, I saw each side of the long tables to which I had been allotted in the Top Hall, filled with some fifty identical faces atop identical Naval uniforms. And was panic-stricken. 'But', I exclaimed in honor, 'I shall never be able to sort them out - they all look alike.' 'You will - they may look alike, but believe me, they are not', confidently assured my guide and guardian angel of those first mazed days. I looked at her sceptically, and yet during those days, watching the smilingly confident ease with which this slim young girl darted about her duties, I slowly began to see a little light.

'Damn it all, you're not a moron,' I told myself and firmly set myself to the task of mastering the intricacies of waitressing, carefully noting any particular feature of my 'charges' as they gave their orders - the red hair for coffee, the wide smile for tea, and a glass of water for that dishy blond American, plus strawberry jam with his breakfast kipper! Beyond that and concentrating on placing the right order in front of the right person and where I had to go for which order, I could spare not a thought - going to bed at night with legs aching and feet sore from the hard stone floors, my head awhirl with spinning tea cups, cascading plates and the mindnumbing fear of spilling a plate of soup over one of those elegant doeskin uniforms. Yet at the end of a month or so, I delightedly found that the computer in my brain was clicking over with a smooth efficiency, and that not only could I confidently fan out several soup dishes and plates, or cups and saucers between my fingers and up my forearms as I sped up and down the long Hall, but that I could do it whilst exchanging lighthearted banter with these suddenly endearing youngsters, thoroughly enjoying the business of the job, and priding myself on giving neat efficient service.

I came to love the centuries-old Painted Hall, entering it always with a feeling of pride and privilege, never ceasing to find pleasure in the richly coloured paintings by the long ago Old Masters that gave it its name, and to study the latter in some quiet off-duty hour; we Wrens would lie on the tables, guidebook in hand, trying to identify the separate pictures.

Hectic days they were, with only a handful of staff to deal with the seemingly endless stream of young officers who came swarming in for their meals, which had to be in two sittings for each meal. Concurrently with this, the other half of my duties lay in looking after the 'cabins' of three or four Senior Naval Officers and the valeting of their persons, the majority of whom had been called back from retirement in order to release younger men to active service. This personal-sounding service turned out to be no more alarming than waking them at 7am with a cup of tea, taking their suits out to brush and their shoes to clean while they drank it, returning with a jug of hot water for shaving (no running H & C, but good oldfashioned basin and ewer, and I regret to say , also chamber pots under the beds.) I would then carefully drape the back of a chair with their clothes in the correct order for donning shoes neatly to attention underneath it, and after giving them a final time check, leave them to it. At first I had been a little apprehensive about all of this, but I need not have been. These august-sounding men, all 'pukka' RN Captains and Commanders, were only older fathers and grandfathers in uniform and I very soon developed an easy friendly rapport with them. I also rather suspected that they quite liked a smiling young girl to wake them in the mornings.

Cabins were cleaned between the serving of breakfast and the attendance at 'Divisions' (the Naval version of School Assembly) and lunch. The afternoons were given to drill lessons under a Royal Marine Sergeant, which greatly pleased my sense of order and love of physical movement; to any necessary pressing of suits, well instructed by a Naval PO, the odd hour or so for personal pursuits and to the setting out of tea things in the various Ward rooms for the officers to help themselves, the latter duty depending on whether I was on or off watch. In the evenings there were the cabin black out curtains to be drawn, beds to be turned down, pyjamas laid out and carafes to be filled with fresh water before going down to the Hall to lay up for and serve at 7.30 dinner.

But hectic though they were, they were also good days despite the bomb-shattered nights, as the enemy planes followed the course of the Thames on which the College stood, dropping bombs both on and all around it. We Wrens at first slept down in the deep stone-built cellars, (more like dungeons) of the College, judiciously segregated from the male Naval personnel who were also crowded down there; then we moved a little higher up under the billiard tables in the Games Rooms, and finally, fed up with never having a proper bed to sleep on, in our own bunks above in the Wren quarters in King Charles block and below the constant explosion of bombs, zooming of aeroplanes and crack of gunfire in the skies above. This was the accompaniment to the dances in the Gun Room when one Captain Johnny Doyle forever requested his favourite Glenn Miller record - *In the Mood* - still resonating loudly over the shocking news of the loss of the *Prince of Wales* and the *Repulse* that rippled round the dance floor on that terrible night in December, bringing us all to a sudden and shaken standstill. All those young lives snatched away, some of whom we had laughed, joked and flirted with only weeks before. It was so difficult for mind and heart to encompass it, and all we could do was to pay them the loving tribute of our silence and our tears.

This was also the time of the incendiary bombs. Little bombs that burst into flames on impact, many of them landing on the roof of the College buildings. The young officers were often kept busy at night dousing with fire hoses. Indeed it was from one such night that my current 'date' came rushing in for breakfast, excitedly waving and shouting 'It's all right Mary - I've saved the tickets!' His quarters were awash, many of his possessions had been burned, he was blearily red-eyed, with smoke-smeared face and uniform, - but the tickets for *Gone with the Wind* (then on its first London run at the Odeon Leicester Square) were safe! Dear Philip M - how I bless him over the years for that. I had read and fallen in love with the book when it first came out and it has been a lifelong companion to me ever since.

At night, as the bombs whistled around, and in answer to a hurried whisper at table of 'Meet me at the West Gate at eight', or a pencilled note passed in the saucer of a cup, we Wrens would cheerfully ignore an 'Alert' to dash through the flak-ridden streets when the day's duties were over, for a visit to the cinema, a meal in the West End, to some dance hall there or at some other Service Unit, or in the College itself. For youth calls to youth and I came to love the rush of these fresh-faced, hungry young men as they came streaming in for their meals, gleefully freed from their classes, high spirits at last uncontained, it never ceasing to give me astonished delight to have my presence greeted with a joyful 'Here she is! Come on Smiler, we're waiting for you!'

Thinking about it at times, I suppose mine was not a very glamorous role to play in the war. But I did not mind. I was neither vain nor ambitious, and was quite content to give of my best as an unglorified waitress-cum-housemaid. Somebody had to do it, it freed a man for active service and, unsure as always of other capabilities I might have, I knew that this at least I could do. More than that, it fulfilled some deep need within me to give of myself (leitmotif, as I later discovered, that ran through all that I have subsequently done) and with my usual zealousness sought to do it as well as I was able.'

CHAPTER 8

THE SECRETS OF RADAR AND PLOTTING

Now as a Third Officer WRNS, and with my tricorne hat at last, I felt very excited to be leaving Greenwich, but also apprehensive of whether I would be capable of plotting, not knowing the first thing about it apart from anticipating the pleasure of scouring secret documents. So, as usual, it was headfirst into the unknown, and fingers crossed.

The Great Western railway line was a joy and I came to know it well; about three or four hours of wonderful English scenery, and with the whole track built by one of my heroes, Isambard Kingdom Brunel. From Exeter, travelling south after the wide river Exe estuary, you snaked along the sweep of coast practically on the beach, while on the inland side there were huge cliffs formed of most attractive good red Devon earth. Every small harbour you passed had busy people doing everything which

Third Officer Oldham - and my tricorne hat at last

exemplified the expression 'messing about in boats', you could also gaze far out to sea and identify liners, tankers and occasional warships plying up and down the Channel. If you were lucky, vast green seas would wash over the whole train.

At Plymouth I had to report to the Superintendent WRNS, Mrs Welby, a well-known and highly thought of lady. In spite of not having the faintest idea what I was to plot, and never having heard of radar at this point, imagine my surprise at finding that I was to be the Plotting Officer in charge of a watch, (of which there were four), in the Commander in Chief's Operations Room overall plot for the whole of Western Approaches. There were four Wren ratings to a watch, working from 1800 to 0900 (fifteen hours), then from 0900 to 1800 the next day, with 48 hours off after that. The Royal Navy and RAF Coastal Command shared this huge operations room at Mount Wise in Plymouth, an area divided into two even halves with a vast map covering the wall at our end, which showed the entire Western Approaches including the whole North Atlantic ocean. At the back of this room and facing the wall map at a raised level, sat the RN and RAF Senior Officers of the day who shared the space - with a glass division to separate them from the Operations Room.

Both the Navy and Coastal Command had their individual radar plots placed in their own halves, consisting of table cabinets with enlarged maps of the west coast and with all the radar stations marked. The maps were covered in transparent talc upon which you could draw routes and write the latest information in coloured wax markers, while small models indicating convoys, ships or aircraft were moved according to the latest information. The four Wrens stood by each of the four sides with headphones on to receive reports.

There were numerous radar stations round these coasts, and the operators would telephone regularly to the Wrens to report the latest position of any ships, convoys or any unidentified blips which appeared on their radar screens, all of which we re plotted immediately. German E-boats were known to try and creep about our coasts; we could therefore be immediately warned of their presence. Aircraft positions were similarly reported to the Coastal Command plot. These positions were marked on the plot so their route, speed and progress could be clearly seen. All the while the plot was consulted by the Officer of the day, by ships' Captains and by visiting Admirals.

Radar to the uninitiated (as I was to learn) means 'Radio Direction and Range' and is a method of detecting the distance and velocity of distant objects, used in military surveillance, air traffic control, marine and air navigation. A trained operator can quickly distinguish the distance of the object, its speed and direction and its consistency.

These details would be telephoned to the Wren who would mark the new information on the plot; thus the operations officers and all concerned could see at a glance the up to the minute position of shipping around the coast. We were taken to visit one of the radar stations at Prawle Point in Devon, which helped one to understand this magic equipment.

I was responsible not only for the radar plot but also for the equally important and thrilling huge wall map which showed the positions of any ship or convoy or reported U-boat in the whole North Atlantic. Information to adjust these came by signal; if there was no new signal information the ship would be moved on according to its supposed speed by dead reckoning. There were slow convoys, usually codenamed ONS (number), with the speed taken from the slowest ship, perhaps 5 knots, and fast convoys of troops, often named HX (number), and special cargoes going at maybe 15 knots. Then there were the 'Monsters', the *Queen Mary, Queen Elizabeth, Mauretania, Aquitania, Franconia,* and others which had been luxury liners, now turned into troop ships.

The convoys were all given zigzag routes of various natures, and these zigzags each had a number with pre-arranged changes of course. When the whole convoy of sixty ships or so, plus the escorts, all changed course at exactly the same moment, it must have been quite a panorama to view, particularly from the air. The convoys would be accompanied by destroyers, corvettes, minesweepers, trawlers or anything else available. Fleet destroyers could do 30-35 knots, the corvettes 12 or thereabouts, and sometimes, in exceptional circumstances, the convoy might be ordered to scatter. I loved this job of keeping the picture bang up to date, and blessed the inspired moment when I had chosen plotting and so luckily been asked to do it; I and my Wrens felt deeply involved watching this horrific but vital Battle of the Atlantic unfold.

Whether anybody but myself knew that I had never been in a plot in my life and had absolutely no idea what I was supposed to do, I never discovered. Plotting was a new category and there was probably no training course suitable at that early part of the war. It was a measure of the confidence placed in one that it could be learned as you went along, without, if possible, causing any major catastrophe. I remember gingerly asking questions of my Wren plotters, trying not to give my ignorance away. The wall map was the most difficult as it was essential to know at what speed the various convoys and ships went, and what their codenames conveyed. Luckily, I had always taken a tremendous interest in all Naval matters and knew the names of every ship in the Fleet, and also what their armament was and the speeds of which they were capable - that helped. I had never been able to forget the splendid sight, viewed from the breakwater of the Grand Harbour in Malta when I was about ten, of the whole Mediterranean Fleet sailing past, which consisted of numerous battleships and battlecruisers, several aircraft carriers - those wonderfully named *Courageous, Glorious and Furious* - many heavy and light cruisers, dozens of destroyers, after which one began to lose count.

If there was a lull during the long night watch we were supposed to go to the canteen and have a bite to eat. This was situated at the main entrance to the building and enabled one to have a breath of fresh air. And for a snooze we were supplied with some rather evil-smelling bunks. However, dozing was always interrupted, very often by an Admiral who would want a chart from the chart cabinet for which I was also responsible. I preferred staying on the job and using any spare time reading, especially as I was deep into Hugh Walpole's Rogue Herries series at the time. Watchkeeping prevented regular sleep for the two days on duty, but forty eight hours off was something to look forward to.

The area of Devonport south of the dockyard, known as Mount Wise, is rich in history and military remains. The dockyard was founded in the 1690s, and during the early 18th century, defensive works known as 'Docklines' were built outside the walls, both encircling them and enclosing an area of housing to the north and Mount Wise to the south. The lines consisted of a wide, deep, dry ditch that ran from Stonehouse creek to the Hamoaze, with a redoubt built at the summit of the ridge that ran across Mount Wise, and a series of gun batteries laid out to protect the dockyard and prevent access to the Hamoaze from Plymouth Sound. This redoubt later became a Naval signal station, equipped with a shutter telegraph connected to the Admiralty in London. A military barracks and laboratory were also built behind the redoubt.

In 1937, as war began to loom again, it was proposed to build in this dry ditch a protected Joint Service Headquarters consisting of a single storey structure with a 20 feet concrete and shingle overburden. By 1939, the plans had widened to provide Area Combined HQs to withstand a direct hit from a 500lb bomb. When you entered this Maritime Headquarters at Mount Wise, you could see the side walls of the dry ditch quite clearly. It was planned to relocate The Naval Command C in C Plymouth and Western Approaches to a safer and more central place, initially on the Clyde and eventually to Liverpool where Derby House had been taken over and strengthened.

We lived in quite reasonable terraced houses out of the town at Mannamead. Public transport in Plymouth was pretty dire at the time. For some reason, all the bus routes seemed to be planned to just miss wherever you were trying to connect. I remember making a vow that if ever I had a chance to revenge myself on a Plymouth bus driver, I would certainly do so. The driver would only have to see you hurrying to catch his bus to put his foot down on the accelerator and speed away, leaving you almost weeping with rage and frustration, standing in the freezing cold gale and hoping something really nasty would overtake him.

By now there were occasional courses laid on for Wrens, and I was sent to do one at Bath. What it was about remains a mystery, but on the return journey I missed my train. How I came to do this I can't imagine, as one of my many failings is always to be frightfully early for everything - no bad thing in my Wren career. This trait I think must be hereditary, as I recall my father describing his family going on a journey by train in his youth. Incredibly, the horse drawn coach, complete with passengers and luggage, was made to do a dress rehearsal to the station the day before. I definitely don't go as far as that, but having missed the train it was a despairing moment, and I could not believe my luck when I was saved by a delightful Polish officer with whom I had been consorting at a party the night before. He astonished me by asking, 'Shall I take you back in the old crate?' 'What old crate?' I asked, and was nearly speechless when I realised he meant by air, and barely managed just to stammer my rapturous acceptance. This episode may sound quite ordinary now, but then it was quite the most daring adventure of my life. My rescuer was, I suppose, an instructor because he had at his disposal a Miles Magister training plane with just two seats one behind the other - in the open air of course. I had to sit on my parachute in the back, and we set off in fine style looking out for, and probably overtaking, the train. My pilot tried to give me some good frights en route and make the trip extra thrilling by dive bombing cows or anything else that took his fancy; I had been hoping that he might loop the loop for an extra show off, but perhaps it was as well that he didn't or I might have fallen out! Flying in an open plane, low down over the river Tamar, and seeing the whole estuary and coast as on a map was an experience I like to relive even today.

There were lots of parties in Plymouth, many of them in ships. As a child I always loved going on board, when my father had been Captain of one of the very distinctive three-funnelled County Class cruisers, HMS *Shropshire*, in the Mediterranean. Everything was terribly cheap in those days in Malta between the wars, and we lived in Guardamangia in some style with a Maltese cook, maids, and a governess to teach my sister, younger brother and me. We even had a chauffeur called Edward, though he did have bare feet. For our riding lessons we went by Carrozzi, (horse drawn Garry), always with the same driver Carlo, who took us cross country at about six in the morning, to the Marsa Polo Club where I learned to ride on David Niven's polo pony; he was out there in Malta before he became a film star, as a young officer in the HLI (the Highland Light Infantry) but my sister Anne and I were only 10 and 11 at the time, and I have always regretted not being a bit older when we could really have appreciated the Fleet at our disposal, not to mention David Niven himself. No-one will ever have better children's parties than the Navy. Sailors simply loved them, and would dress up as pirates and give us rides in the lifts which brought up ammunition for the huge 8 inch guns.

The parties I went to as a Wren in Plymouth were of a very different calibre, but they were never to be forgotten and we made friends with some amazing submariners, many of whom were based there. This was my first real introduction to the secret, underwater, dangerous world; one which seems to attract a unique and brave breed of man. Submarine crews are the pick of the Navy, for this highly specialised service offers fine opportunities for individual derring-do - the dauntless spirit that animated our famous sailors of old. They are the hidden eyes and ears of the Navy, able to lurk undetected, observing enemy movements and able to hear the slightest, distant whirr of machinery by catching the sound waves, using the hull of the submerged submarine as a giant hydrophone. (This acts rather on the principle of a stethoscope).

Parties in submarines were particularly special, as apart from the excitement of actually going on board one of these esoteric vessels, space was at a premium and the tiny ward room was very cosy. Whenever possible on Saturday nights, we would be invited for drinks on board, before going on to Genonis - an Italian restaurant near Drake's Circus, or to the Moreland Links Hotel out near Yelverton where we danced the night away. We always wore long evening dresses, although my friend Eve Lindsay and I had very few of these and used to borrow from each other to ring the changes. Another friend was Ruby Cortez who had been secretary to the film magnate Alexander Korda - she was a ball of fire. One famous evening, Steve, who was the Paymaster on board, suggested that as we were so tired of our same old dresses, why not wear their dinner jackets for a change? This brilliant idea took some organising and it is impossible to imagine the contortions necessary when they tied our bow ties.

Lennox Napier was the Captain of our host ship, HMS *Rorqual*, a big minelaying submarine, and had just returned from two years active service in the Mediterranean. He became a great friend and as

HMS Rorqual

well as spending these entertaining evenings together, we used to walk miles over Dartmoor discussing everything under the sun; we never came to any conclusion about the future, which seemed far away and insecure, but somehow I thought that when the war was won and if we were both still alive, we would meet again. I always felt he came from that rather romantic genre who would not commit himself to any course of action he could not be sure of carrying out. He rarely talked about what he had been doing; it was all very hush-hush and although I knew what a distinguished war he had had, I only discovered some of the details when he died recently. This is from one of his several obituaries:

'Lennox Napier won both the DSO and the DSC in recognition of his gallant and skilful conduct of unusual operations in command of the submarine *Rorqual* in the Mediterranean between June 1941 and December 1943. One of her major tasks was to ferry supplies to the beleaguered island of Malta, (known as 'Magic Carpet' runs). Built as a minelayer with rails and a chain conveyor belt, enclosed by a casing on her deck, *Rorqual* was an awkward and bulky submarine and was the only one of her class to survive the war. Her tonnage was 1,520 and at 280 ft long, beam 29ft, - her very size made her invaluable - and on her

Lennox Napier at sea

first voyage to Malta she carried a vital cargo of two tons of medical supplies, 62 tons of high octane aviation spirit for the RAF Hurricanes, 45 tons of cooking fuel and 25 passengers, as well as 147 bags of much appreciated mail. *Rorqual* laid a total of 1,599 mines, up to 50 at a time, and Napier's skill in laying them, often in the crystal clear waters of the Mediterranean, brought him a number of successes. One of these was the valuable German heavy-lift ship

Ankara loaded with tanks for Rommel's Afrika Corps. He then sank an enormous tanker, followed immediately by the steamer *Wilhelmsburg*, after which it was reported that his exploits prompted Hitler to lose his temper with Grand Admiral Karl Donitz - an accolade he valued almost as much as his DSO and DSC.'

One of his less successful ventures was a carrier pigeon trial, which failed as the birds refused to leave the boat. Another not entirely fruitful idea was to turn day into night, as it was only safe to surface at night, better use might be made of the opportunities.

Lennox was a descendant of John Napier, the inventor of Napierian logarithms and the decimal point - and after the war he read Mathematics at the Open University. Lennox was also a brilliant linguist, and even went ashore when serving on the China station before the war and lived with a Chinese family to learn the language. He married twice and his first wife, Eve Lindsay, was my great friend.

We corresponded after I left Plymouth and he went back to the Mediterranean, and shortly I shall reproduce some of these epic letters which arrived from time to time, and which included a few cryptic clues of his whereabouts and what he was up to. He was a considerable artist and they are illustrated in his inimitable style; to me, they are gems of prose.

CHAPTER 9

⚓

LENNOX'S LETTERS
AND THE SILENT SERVICE

A mystery, which after sixty years I cannot unravel in spite of racking my brains, is how exactly I fitted in two other appointments between Plymouth and Belfast. For some unfathomable reason I was sent to Edinburgh for plotting duties and to be the Naval Liaison officer at Turnhouse, now the main airport of that city. I had to live in a hotel in the town which had its advantages, but it was quite a long journey to work, albeit transported by very comfortable white trams. I remember feeling frightfully ill one day, but my room was up about a million stairs at the very top of the hotel building, and the idea of going down to telephone was so arduous it actually seemed easier to go to work and tell them how ill I felt when I got there. After a few days of this my mother happened to visit, and asked me why my face was bright red and covered in spots. She immediately diagnosed German measles. The hotel manager was not frightfully pleased, and my mother and I were marooned in the top of the building until I recovered. I was quite ill with this unpredictably violent illness, and went home to recuperate. I never warmed to anything about my next appointment to Newcastle-on-Tyne, where after getting very lost among the yellow trolley-buses and finding the watches not at all to my taste, I put in for a transfer almost at once. I had never been to Ireland, and when I was offered a return to Plymouth or Belfast I chose the latter. All my friends had left Plymouth, and this was still Western Approaches. I found I had missed the firsthand knowledge of all that was going on in the Atlantic. By now, however, I was beginning to get a series of very cheering up letters from the Mediterranean.

Letters were unbelievably important during the war, and one

longed for the arrival of mail. There were few telephones and one was rarely allowed to use them for personal calls which always had to be pre-arranged; unlike today when everyone is immediately accessible by mobile, and ringing up all your nearest and dearest at least five times a day is normal practice. During the war, people simply did not think like that, and even owning a telephone was by no means universal. Friends were of the essence, in fact one's lifeblood. You were rarely stationed near any relations or contacts, and arriving at some unknown, God forsaken and bleak outpost of Empire, as it seemed, breaking the ice at a new appointment was often a lonely business. With no telephone or e-mail, letters were the only way of communicating; we really did write and enjoy writing lots of letters to all our friends and relations, it was so important to keep in touch, and to receive a nice, long, newsy and gossipy letter was the greatest treat and one would re-read it a dozen times. The post was also terribly slow, partly because it all had to come via London, having to be addressed to HMS....c / o GPO London.

Lennox's first letter arrived while he was still at Plymouth, and ended with the following:

'I hope you are going to write to me from time to time. This is good for morale of persons in Foreign Parts and even if distasteful, may be counted as war work and therefore highly virtuous. Besides it is a pity when one just disappears into the blue, I think.

I have a terrible 'end of the holidays' feeling these last few days here and shall be glad to be gone, Love Lennox.'

His second one was also from Plymouth, undated, and his address was HMS *Rorqual* c/o GPO London.

'My dear Christian,

This is to wish you a final farewell - Empire or otherwise according to taste. 'Ave atque vale', as we say in our usual affected manner. (This has got in because I have been reading Tacitus - about that dear Mr Caligula, such a nice man).

You might hardly credit it but I went off yesterday evening, being Saturday, to a certain well-known hotel with Steve, Eve, Ruby and others; this time really was the last though. It gives me particular pleasure to be able to announce that on returning, Ruby in person was soundly censured by one of her angry messmates for making too much noise.

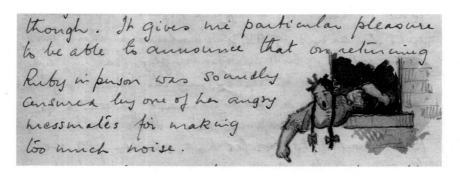

though. It gives me particular pleasure to be able to announce that on returning Ruby in person was soundly censured by one of her angry messmates for making too much noise.

Don't imagine however that we have been here enjoying the flesh-pots ever since you left. We have been places in the meanwhile. One place we went was both unintentional and dramatic. We were steaming through a certain Narrow and Rocky Place with a local Pilot in charge. While passing the lighthouse so close that the lighthousekeeper not only could, but did, spit on to the upper deck, we suddenly began to go sharply uphill and finally came to a rest with a grinding crunch. At this point the pilot, with the famous last words 'Oh xxxx it' on his lips, passed clean away into the arms of the Sublieutenant, who, taken by surprise, fell backwards into the arms of the Signalman, thus most successfully, but unsportingly, leaving me with the onus of extricating the whole organisation from a predicament for which he was entirely responsible. This we managed. But the Pilot's bowler hat, which fell over the side in the general turmoil, was last seen being worn by a

porpoise, disporting itself round the ship's bows. At least so a Leading Stoker declared, though the man in question is notoriously unreliable. The beast he said had exceptionally beautiful eyelashes.

This morning I was paid a final visit by some of the Old Guard, who were shown round the boat, so choc-a-bloc with boxes and stores, trunks, potatos, and pistons that after an extended obstacle race, with all participants glowing freely at the end of it, I do not really think they had seen anything at all. Ruby said afterwards that now she under-stood why people found service in submarines so absorbing. So Heaven

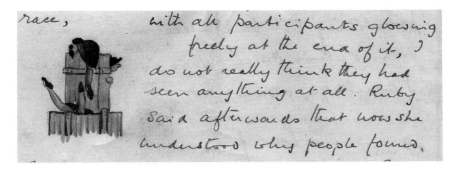

race, with all participants glowing freely at the end of it, I do not really think they had seen anything at all. Ruby said afterwards that now she understood why people fainted,

knows what idea she has got into her head or is now going to spread about in an unsuspecting world.

I take it that by this time, your two Commanders, if not the RAF, will have been set well on the road to being brought to heel. I cannot help hoping they are that type of Commander you have been used to dealing with in these parts. This kind - if you catch my meaning.

A man is practising the banjulele in the next room of this hotel. This is too much - I can't go on.

Love Lennox.'

The next letter took about seven months to arrive during a period of the war when all shipping was routed round the Cape: He starts by saying:

'After setting out on its travels about Sept 22nd, this letter has circumnavigated Africa and reached me again circa April 15th, in an envelope somewhat embarrassingly addressed 'Lennox' HMS Rorqual. As, however, I am incurably lazy, I have no compunction whatever on sending it off once more on its way, thus relieving me of the necessity of thinking of anything new to say. Besides it still appears to me a fine piece of English prose and you might as well know what we were at in September. Suffice it to say we are in no Arcadia now.

Love Lennox.'

If he ever explained from where this next letter was written, I have forgotten, but it could just be the Lebanon, which he refers to again in a later letter. He continues:

'We are now installed in our new home - and very nice it is, I must say. We live in a large and commodious house, once the property of Russian hermits. I must confess I had always imagined hermits to be austere, ascetic gentlemen, living in caves in the mountains. But not at all. Asceticism is strikingly absent from the home and the flesh is only seriously mortified by the marked inadequacy of the bathing arrangements - a state of affairs which I strongly suspect did not mortify the Russians in the least.

One other cross indeed we do have to bear and that is the immediate proximity of a large contingent of the so called Fighting French. There appears to be only one important aspect of French Military Training and that is bugling. At 0500 it starts with the instructor playing 'do' - then every recruit plays 'do', some a little sharp, some a little flat' Then the instructor plays 'do do' and the recruits follow suit.*

> *at 0500 it starts with the instructor playing ♪ — then every recruit plays ♪, some a little sharp + some a little flat. Then the instructor plays ♪♪ and the recruits follows suit. All day long. with no pause, they stick at it, until about 1900 they have reached [musical notation] after which, thank God, they stop. And so to work again at 0500*

All day long with no pause they stick at it, until about 1900 they have reached 'do do do do' 4 times, after which thank God they stop.

And so to work again at 0500 the next morning. But what after all does that matter when we are living in lovely country, where rationing is unheard of (by us), where I am supplied with a motor car and chauffeur at the public expense, and where in between patrols, I am sent to cool off 3,000 ft up in the mountains.

French is the language of our daily intercourse. This comes a trifle hard anyway after long years of disuse, but what really upsets me is that I am informed not by one person or by two but by all whom I meet, that I speak the language with the most perfect German accent. However since no-one here has heard more than vague rumours of there being some kind of a war, or at least some marked divergence of opinion between the powers in the great world outside, this does not really matter.

Truly the people, at least the village people round about, are almost embarrassingly friendly. As one goes for one's Saturday afternoon walk in the hills one is pressed on every side - to go into this cottage for a cup of coffee or to accept a great bunch of grapes from the vine growing over the door of that one. In short, we live in a kind of Arcadia with Bugling. What of course makes it even more Arcadian for me at the moment is that on the second day in harbour my entire wardrobe was removed from the clothes line by an enterprising burglar while the laundryman was engaged in enjoying his siesta. The simplicity of attire compelled by this disaster should perhaps be called Spartan rather than Arcadian and in any case is not altogether unsuited to the climate.

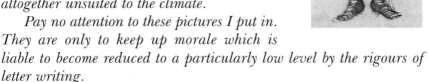

Pay no attention to these pictures I put in. They are only to keep up morale which is liable to become reduced to a particularly low level by the rigours of letter writing.

Naturally in this Eden there must be Nymphs and Shepherdesses and what have you. The best we can do in this line at present is a small female cypher staff who live in our mess. This I must tell you at once does not add all it might to the above idyllic scene, chiefly on account of the local General's wife - a charming lady no doubt, but one whose continual presence in the wardroom fills me with the utmost alarm and despondency. Particularly is this so since there is no way of getting from my cabin to the bathroom except by going through the mess. The

disadvantages of this layout are apparent, and as I scurry past furtively on my way to my evening scrub, loofah in hand and all too inadequately clad for communing with Generals' wives, I get the iciest stare from the good lady who has a most unhappy predilection for a seat immediately outside my door.

I am afraid you may hardly believe me when I tell you that we have now really acquired a violin for our wardroom (a present from a gentleman who could not take all his baggage home, which he insisted on pressing on my Engineer Officer in spite of the most vehement protestations that he had no use for the instrument). 'The Bluebells of Scotland' has so far been practised only (and that, pizzicato, owing to restrictions of space which make bowing difficult) and it has been decided that only performances of this classic are to be reserved for the occasions of our operational successes, when it will be rendered by myself as a kind of paean on the ancient Greek model. As a matter of fact we have had a slight opening success, but by the time the depth charges had ceased pattering about our ears, it must be confessed that 'The Bluebells' had come to be somewhat overlooked. Next time however, there shall be no mistake.

I know you are in fact keeping my morale up as promised and that it is simply ill fortune that all your letters get sunk or shot down en route. (As a matter of fact, as I have not had a single letter since we left home, I am not really complaining at all).

Wishing you in conclusion a Merry Michaelmas and a Happy Lord Mayor's Day.

Lots of Love, Lennox.'

The next letters all came in the form of Airmail Letter Cards, which when folded twice, formed a normal envelope size. The instructions said, 'When folded, the Letter Card must conform in size and shape with the blue border within which the address only may be written.'

One dated 10th Feb begins:

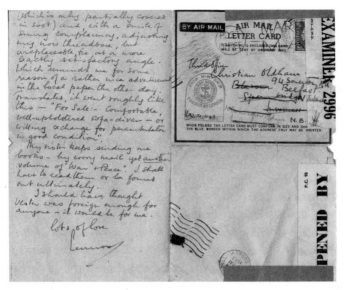

'My dear Christian,

How nice to hear of you after all these months. I have just got a letter from you - dated 14th September! - nevertheless this leads me to hope there may be others, spread around in space-time, which will be rolling in slowly, but steadily, long after the outbreak of peace.

I wonder if my letters to you, of which I must ask you to believe there have been several, are also arriving after a similar interval, or at all, for they have all been addressed to Edinburgh, where I suppose you have not been at all. Never mind, it is the kind thought which is really important they say.

We have long since left that Garden of Eden in which we started our career abroad and are now in very sorry though slowly improving quarters. Such trifling things as the rain coming through the roof, a total lack of hot water are such everyday matters that they are no longer noticed. I have however been provided with a new cabin. Into this, by a most ingenious arrangement, is blown a continuous shower of soot through an inaccessible ventilator which takes its supply from a neighbouring chimney. Life in fact is exactly like a continuous residence in a dismal railway station in which there is only corned beef and dry bread in the buffet and the conveniences are out of order. The austerity of our daily fare was well summed up the other day by a sailor, *who I happened to overhear as he finished his tinned plums, which had formed part of his lunch, and who by means of the stones endeavoured to ascertain what he was going to get for supper. As he pushed each stone to the side of his plate he was reciting 'Corned beef, pressed beef, turned beef, beef'.*

The chief incident of our last patrol, however, must not be over-looked, which was that the rats successfully gnawed right through the coxswain's braces while he was asleep. As we have now a kind of blood-sucking bug on board to add to our old friends, the rats, cockroaches, fleas and wood-lice, the struggle for existence is becoming one of ever growing intensity.

You might suppose that I am having a moan and that morale is bad. On the contrary, it is very good (touching wood) the war has not been going too badly for me lately and you may even have seen some highly garbled accounts of our doings in the press.

Yesterday I had to go and lecture on Submarine Warfare to a large party of soldiers. On arriving on the platform the local military chieftain introduced me as Lieut-Colonel Napier which completely unnerved me and left the whole audience tittering. Later I told a grossly exaggerated funny story of one of our one-time soldier passengers, only to discover too late that he was MO (Medical Officer) of the Regiment, and actually in the audience. He now keeps coming to our Mess and asking for me - oh dear. There is precious little room on these damn things (these bits of paper, I mean). I will write you a better letter later.

Lots of love, Lennox.'

The next letter is dated 29th March. (As he rarely puts the year after the date, and I can't remember, the reader must be somewhat baffled by the sequence of events. Much of this narrative happened simultaneously during the first years of the war, so the chronology may not be entirely clear.)

'My dear Christian,

How satisfactory that we have at last established communication. I should have a great deal to tell you about the last six months really, but, alas I can never do it, for fear that another letter may turn up with a totally different version of the same story. The deplorable habit of improving events for publication may in such cases find one out.

You may hardly believe it, but since I last wrote to you I have had three days of the most glorious skiing. This in a country which I have already described to you at some length (vide my 17. 10. 42, now about at Cape Town) and which is an absolute heaven in this troubled world. For not only can one go skiing, but almost every other human pleasure is provided - you can stuff yourself to the epiglottis with everything that you had almost forgotten about, I expect, from oranges to oysters, the shops are full and the countryside is one of the most beautiful places I have ever seen. Below the snow line the flowers are almost beyond belief although spring had hardly begun - solid masses of poppies between the olive trees, gentians, anemones, wild cyclamen and cherry, and God knows how many I have no idea of the name of. Now we are back in the hard world again after only four days of this, but at least every corner of the submarine is packed to capacity with chocolate, razor blades, ivory, apes and peacocks against the bad times to come. I cannot forbear to repeat one item of news. That is that we acquired a violin, a present from a fleeing evacuee, and on Christmas Day I gave a stirring rendering of 'The Bluebells' in the presence of my Petty Officers, meanwhile my Gunlayer, a more competent fiddler than myself, persisted in playing 'The Road to the Isles' under the slightly alcoholic impression that he was accompanying me. Probably very bad for discipline, but I think no-one had any very clear recollection of the events next day. This is perfectly true - there was no luverly blonde present.

Lots of love, Lennox.'

This is the last of his letters, the only material items apart from my Wren officer's cap badge that I have as souvenirs from the war. I had completely forgotten about them until I started to write this book, and now I find they portray vividly, through a porthole as it were, the picture of half a relationship. One never forgets old friends such as these.

CHAPTER 10

—— ⚓ ——

TO SEA IN A SUBMARINE

I can only imagine the sheer amazement and shock on the face of a hardened Submarine Captain such as Lennox Napier, having been selected to attend the legendary 'Perishers' course at his headquarters HMS *Dolphin* at Fort Blockhouse, Gosport, the hub of all such boats, only to find he was to be instructed by what he would consider 'a chit of a girl', a Leading Wren, and her small team. The 'Perishers' course was the acme of a submariner's career; even if an experienced Commanding Officer already, he was still handpicked for this highly esteemed refresher course for the newest, up-to-the-moment techniques, or as a potential candidate for such a position. Commanding Officers of submarines were placed under intense pressure, and tested to their mental, physical and psychological limits. The candidate's astonishment would be quickly replaced by surprised respect for the remarkable capability of the girls, and the success of the experiment for Wrens to replace seamen. These girls had been trained by Commander HF Bone, a renowned Submarine Commander himself, who first had the idea that Wrens could replace male instructors and man the control table at the Attack Teacher, (a simulator). Commander Howard Francis Bone RN had made the name HMS *Tigris* feared in enemy circles by sinking eleven ships with an aggregate displacement of 38,500 tons, for which he was awarded the DSO and Bar and the DSC and Bar.

Surely these remarkable Wrens' achievements in Attack Teacher must have been the pinnacle of endeavour for Wrens replacing sailors.

Hazel Russell (Hough) was introduced to me when I was on my

quest for wartime Wrens who had experienced interesting careers. I asked if she had ever told her unique story to anyone before, and she said no-one had ever been interested. Also, of course, when one was sworn to secrecy for years after the war, you had almost forgotten yourself what had happened so long ago. Here is what she says:

'In 1941 I was twenty one and a fully trained secretary, employed by an insurance company. In my spare time I drove a YMCA van to anti-aircraft gun and balloon defence sites in

Hazel Russell (Hough)

the north London area. Since I wanted to join the Services I decided to volunteer to join the WRNS and hoped that I could become a driver. I was accepted and arrived in Portsmouth in September to do two weeks general training.

I was then given a driving test and to my surprise was told that I had failed and they tried to persuade me to become a typist.

HMS *Dolphin*, the submarine base in Portsmouth harbour, had a simulator known as the Attack Teacher and fortunately they were considering the possibility of recruiting six Wrens to replace the sailors who manned it. The Attack Teacher was used to complete the training of First Lieutenants to become 'Perishers' (trained Captains), and experienced Captains went back to learn the latest tactics and details of potential targets. The normal male crew was to be posted to sea and the plan was to find out whether Wrens could replace them, and I with one other girl was chosen to see whether after three weeks training we could take over. The instructor, Commander HF Bone, a very distinguished submarine Captain, decided we were competent, and I, having been made Leading Wren, together with five other Wrens, became the crew in November 1941.

The simulator was housed in a building on the *Dolphin* quay and had two floors; the lower one known as the control room had a rotating conning tower with a periscope and various instruments including a gramophone playing underwater noises. The most important instrument was the 'fruit machine' - a m e chanical analogue computer, which was fed with target information, submarine depth etc, and worked out the torpedo firing conditions. The upper floor had mechanisms to control the movement of the model targets along

Teaching Submarine Attack. Hazel is on the right side of the picture taking instruction from the control room below. The target ship comes in on the 'railway', which is being controlled by the other Wren.

a rail track some fifty yards long. In addition in this room there was a large plotting table on which the torpedo tracks were recorded for critical analysis. The models were all very tiny but accurate replicas of enemy shipping, and were kept up to date throughout the war and of course, were subject to tight security.

The whole complex was Top Secret and had to be manned at night by two Wrens which meant that I slept on board every third night. There was, in addition to the main room on the lower floor where the courses were carried out, a small room which contained t wo camp beds and ve ry limited facilities. This was our accommodation which we used generally and when we were on 'watch'. The *Dolphin* canteen was a considerable distance away, and when on duty we sometimes preferred to turn our electric stove on its back and heat soup and make scrambled eggs made from tinned egg powder.

The Officers' training lasted six weeks, three with us at the AT and the other three at sea. During the three weeks before the next course arrived we carried out all the maintenance; the cleaning, polishing and scrubbing necessary to satisfy our very critical Commander. This work was carried out by the six Wrens, as no other personnel were allowed into the facility. These three weeks were also when leave was taken, and in addition we were available to carry out other duties to help the Establishment.

When the new course arrived the Commander addressed them and told them they were about to learn the very latest technique to be used in carrying out an attack on an enemy ship. This covered the approach to a firing position which was recorded on the plotting table in detail, together with the actual firing point of the torpedoes, and after each attack was made, the results were analysed and discussed.

At the end of each course, Commander Bone expected the officers to take us six Wrens out to dinner over the water to Southsea, to show their appreciation of the hard work and support we had given them on their course. On one occasion when we missed the *Jolly Boat* back, and were locked out of our quarters at Alverstoke, we were punished by having to peel potatoes for three weeks.

When *Taku*, a T Class submarine, came to *Dolphin* and her officers attended our refresher course, they were invited to a dance at our quarters at Alverstoke. During the evening we chided them, saying that we Wrens, having been through dozens of attacks, could achieve more hits on enemy targets than they could. They answered jokingly, 'Why don't you come out to sea and show us?' I replied that we would like the challenge, but when their Captain, Commander Pitt, was asked for permission, he laughed and said that if it was sanctioned from above, he would gladly take us! The next day, I approached Commander Bone, who agreed that we deserved to go, but said that I would have to see Admiral Darke, the Commanding Officer of *Dolphin* and get his agreement. I then saw the Chief Wren Officer who obtained an appointment with him. When the day arrived I was extremely nervous, but the Admiral put me at ease and said that he had received glowing reports of our work, and that he would give his agreement providing we strictly adhered to his conditions. These were: that the exercise would be Top Secret; that we would embark before daylight and on returning would disembark in a discreet manner; and for obvious reasons would wear bell-bottom trousers.

Number One, (the First Officer) of *Taku*, who made all the rearrangements necessary for his crew of about fifty men to accommodate us on a temporary basis, greeted us six rather nervous Wrens aboard before the sun rose. We were made very welcome and soon got used to the odours and cramped conditions. Commander Pitt arrived and we cast off and sailed down the Solent, on the surface, out into the English Channel. We were given a tour of the boat and saw all that went on in each department, and I was enormously impressed by the size of the torpedoes. We then spent a lot of time in the control room, where we were much more familiar with the equipment.

We cruised around on the surface waiting for the target ship to arrive for the torpedo firing exercise, and during this wait each Wren went up into the conning tower and looked out across the water for any signs of activity. When our target arrived in the exercise area, we dived to periscope depth which was about twenty five feet. In turn, we each looked through the periscope at the target and, with the ship's crew casting a watchful eye on us, we assisted the Number One Officer to carry out the first attack. When he fired the dummy torpedo it was a direct hit. Then I took over and manoeuvred the boat into a firing position and fired. The first torpedo missed, but the second was a hit, and I shouted 'Down periscope!', and the Captain took us down to 'safety'. Everyone was delighted with the result of the exercise.

We then surfaced, and the officers gave up their tiny wardroom for us to have a tot and a splendid lunch. The Captain told us that the CPO chef had spent the entire morning organising a sumptuous meal of roast beef, Yorkshire pudding and vegetables followed by an exotic sweet. After thanking the Captain and his officers for taking us out and giving us such a thrilling day, we returned to base, tired but very pleased to have had the privilege of going to sea in a submarine. And when finally ashore, we swore to keep secret our special exercise, and what we had seen in one of Her Majesty's operational submarines.

Working with these officers meant that we Wrens knew them well by the end of the three weeks, and had a good understanding of the dangers they were about to face. Normally they went into combat waters when they left us, and naturally their leaving left us concerned. The loss of one of our boats, especially if it had been captained by one of our course members, was a thoroughly depressing event for us.'

Hazel persuaded all of her 'Perishers' to sign the copy of her book *Up Periscope* by David Masters, which she has kept as a memorable souvenir. She and her team must be among very few Wrens to have had such a wonderful chance; I can't imagine anything more thrilling than to actually go to sea, submerge in an operational submarine, and then be able with all her experience and training to fire the torpedo and hit, and finally to be allowed to give the order 'Down periscope!' It must have been the apogee of her ambitions.

Hazel persuaded all of her 'Perishers' to sign the copy of her book 'Up Periscope' by David Masters.

CHAPTER 11

⚓

IRELAND

While digging into my recollections of my time in Northern Ireland, I remembered several friends, but could I remember their names? One I found in a very old address book, Betty Cruddas (Ashcroft), and thinking it unlikely she was still at the same address, I rang telephone enquiries to see if there was anyone of that name still in her village. By great good luck there was, so I rang the number, and lo and behold it was Betty herself, and she remembered me! Not bad after sixty years or so. She was able to enlighten me on several points, and better still, put me on to another mutual friend with whom she was still in touch - Norrisse Whitehead (Ford). Norrisse elated me further by saying she thought she had a group photograph, with me in it, in my uniform. I had quite given up hope of such a record existing - which she duly produced.

The Royal Navy had chosen Belfast Castle to install their Headquarters, which overlooked the city from a prominent site 400 feet above sea level on the slopes of Cave Hill. The edifice was originally built by the Normans in the late 12th century and in 1611 a stone and timber building was erected by Sir Arthur Chichester, Baron of Belfast,

Norrisse Whitehead's photograph of the author, front row far right, positively in her hat!

which sadly burned down in 1708. The Chichesters lived in England until the 19th century when the 3rd Marquis of Donegall built a new residence within the Deer Park on Cave Hill, following the Scottish baronial style of architecture, which had become fashionable after Balmoral was built by Queen Victoria in 1853.

Ireland was quite an eye opener. There was no shortage of food, and we lived very well in our communal Wren quarters. These were opposite the police station which was filled with tall, young and good-looking constables, all eager to help us and escort us through the rather dark path which separated us. The border was very close, and could always be relied upon to supply us with anything we could not obtain in Ulster. The Royal Navy ships, many of them based there, would often stock up with so called 'rabbits' - scarce or luxurious or forbidden objects - to cheer up their next convoy escort duty. Norrisse and Betty and I would make occasional sorties to Dublin by train, where rationing of any sort was not a problem. One would buy a ration book at Dublin Station (the Irish are always so practical about these matters) and off we would go to buy everything we could afford, and of which we had been deprived by the shortages at home. In fact we had a meal every two hours or so, to make sure we had as much steak and cream as we could fit in. We bought birthday and Christmas presents as if there were no tomorrow; and the shops were full of the most tempting clothes. There was only one snag - the customs. These were very strict, and everything we bought had to be smuggled. There were several stations where the train stopped on our way to and fro, and on the return journey the customs officers' favourite sport was to come on board the train at every station and catch us at it. It was always a difficult decision if you had purchased a new garment, whether to wear it and risk being taken off the train and searched, or screw it up in the suitcase to make it look worn. If this did happen, and it frequently did, you were liable to miss the train home and be adrift. Our best and most successful trick was to hang the shopping bag on the outside door handle on the off-side of the train, but this was risky too, and of course we also stuffed things down our bras, up our sleeves and could also sit on flattish parcels - once I successfully sat on a box of cigars.

Our plot was similar to the one in Plymouth, but more a strategic plot than an operational one. The Commander in Chief had moved his operations room from Plymouth to Liverpool, while we in Belfast were kept informed of everything that was happening by signal and teleprinter so we had an accurate and up-to-date picture for visiting officers. Our own radar plot recorded the many ships coming up the Irish Sea and from Liverpool and Glasgow, to assemble for the huge slow convoys or the smaller faster ones which formed up to the north, off the west coast of Scotland near a rocky outcrop called Rockall. Many of the escort ships, destroyers, corvettes and minesweepers were based at Londonderry, and would chase around the vast array of merchant ships like trial sheepdogs, getting them organised in time to sail. A slow convoy might have as many as sixty ships with two or three corvettes and perhaps one destroyer; there would have to be complete blackout, and sometimes if a slow convoy, a speed of no more than five knots - that of the slowest ship.

1942 was the worst year for the Atlantic Battle. While we were slowly getting better at protecting our indispensable cargoes, the Germans were improving their U-boat wolf pack tactics. The RAF provided air cover for the first part of the crossing, and the Royal Canadian Air Force would attempt the same from their side as far as the range permitted, but as the ships reached the Black Hole, or Air Gap as it was known, (about thirty degrees west, and too far for the longest ranged Liberator to patrol) the U-boats had learned to wait, and they did not have to wait long. The endless black nights and the terrible weather loaded the dice towards our enemy. In our castle plot, we moved the shipping on their known course and speed with the greatest anxiety, dreading the first signal which announced a U-boat sighting or attack. Worse still, we knew and worried about many of the escorts and their crews.

It was late in that year of 1942 that I arrived in Belfast and was plunged into many of those frightful arenas that we saw from a distance, but in which we felt an intimate part. We worked high up in the castle, which had a fine view of Belfast Lough and could observe our ships coming and going. The radar plot was in the middle of the room, and there was a wall plot of the Western Approaches and the whole Atlantic as there had been in Plymouth. Next door to us and connected by a hatch was the cypher room and the cypher officers, where Norrisse was in charge, and they handed all the signals through to us as they came in and when they had been uncoded. The valuable Pink List was available through the hatch as well. There was always a Senior Naval Officer of the day (also working in watches) for us to consult, and I particularly recall a certain night when one of them, who always slept soundly on the floor under his desk, was absolutely impossible to wake up, and this night there was a real emergency. A ship coming north was steering far too close to the shore. I wanted to send it a warning signal of its dangerous position, and required his authority to do so. We pulled him out, sat him up, patted his face, even threw water over him, but he slept on - so I sent the signal anyway.

HMS Oribi

Ships of the escorts returning from convoy duty to Londonderry were sometimes sent to Belfast for repairs, and on such a chance occasion a Fleet destroyer, HMS *Oribi*, of the Tribal Class came in with storm damage.

It goes without saying that she had her Naval priorities correctly aligned, and one of her first actions was to send to Belfast Castle for a contingent of Wrens to join the ward room just as soon as the sun was over the yardarm. There was no lack of volunteers, and I was among those who went on this blind date which had lifelong consequences for me. In fact, this was the start of a whirlwind romance which ended

Lieutenant John Lamb DSC RN

ten days later with my becoming engaged to the first lieutenant, Lieutenant John Bruce Lamb DSC Royal Navy.

Naturally this called for a monumental party, and John, in his capacity as President of the Wardroom Mess, decreed a Guest Night Dinner. Invitations were sent to all my Wren friends, and all ships' officers had to wear dinner jackets in honour of the occasion. The Wardroom stewards laid on a stupendous menu which I am sure included steak and kidney pie and probably plum duff for pudding - both Naval favourites, washed down with plenty of Pink Gins, White Ladies, Gimlets and Dry Martinis. The ritual of the dinner concluded with clearing the table and passing the port, after which the loyal toast and many other toasts were made to the newly engaged couple, the Captain and his wife, absent wives and girlfriends, the nearest Admiral and so on. After this, traditional high jinks were the order of the day, and those who declined to participate wedged themselves securely out of harm's way. First came a game of Wardroom Polo, ridden on chairs, with spoons as sticks and one of the remaining potatos as the ball. After further refreshment all round, the indoor torpedo was fired with all the appropriate drill recited by the gunner, the missile being the midshipman who was projected the length of the shiny dining room table at the target which was the settee at the end. Finally, with everyone well lubricated, the Obstacle Race took place, when they all had to circumnavigate the wardroom without touching the deck. This ended with lights out because of the blackout, with the participants having to squeeze through the ship's side scuttle, climb over the top and in again by the other side. This of course made people very thirsty - again.

John kept various diaries, and in co-ordinating these into his memoirs years later, he wrote, 'In the fourteen days it took Harland and Wolfe to patch us up I met and became engaged to Christian Oldham, my wife today. She was then a Third Officer WRNS in charge of a watch at Maritime Headquarters and was among a party of Wren Officers invited to drinks in the Wardroom on our first night in harbour - so in true Naval style no time was wasted. Her girls, who called themselves 'The Hags Watch,' insisted on sending me this reference stamped:

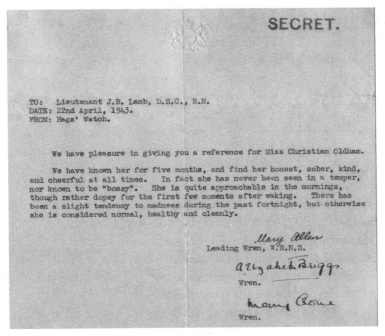

John had won his Distinguished Service Cross when his ship HMS *Glasgow* was torpedoed off Crete, and towed, badly damaged into Alexandria harbour. It was early in 1941, the moment of the first real British success since the outbreak of the war. Wavell's Western Desert Force, under General O'Connor, spectacularly counter attacked the enemy and pushed them back into Libya, leaving trails of guns, rifles, wrecked vehicles, burned out tanks, and bodies lying where they had fallen, and hundreds of prisoners of war from the battle of Sidi Barrani. I quote again from John's memoirs: 'I could hardly believe my luck when I was told that as the ship was going to be out of action for several months, I was to pack my bag, draw khaki fatigues and take a small communications party up to Sidi Barrani where the army was landing supplies and evacuating prisoners. I was to be Beachmaster, and within hours I was sailing westwards with my three sailors in a naval auxiliary vessel. On arrival it was too rough to land so we transferred to Lighter X39, a relic of the 1915 Dardanelles campaign, which meanwhile had arrived with supplies for the military. After a bitterly cold night we headed for the shore at first light, making slow progress in our clumsy craft which wallowed in the ground swell There were low cliffs above a sandy beach, with yet more sand beyond, varied by dunes and a general rise inland. I organised several hundred prisoners, who appeared from the background to form a chain, and they were soon busy unloading fuel, water and provisions. I then set off with a guide to report to the local army commander at his headquarters, some way inland. We passed through the wrecked village, a cluster of buildings on top of a hill, like a small citadel, not a soul to be seen, until we came to an inconspicuous hummock in the sand; in reply to my guide's 'Hulloa', a military looking head rose neck high, like a Djinn of the magic lamp, and beckoned me down into an ancient Egyptian tomb, where a Brigadier and his staff were working in this ready-made bomb proof shelter which was their HQ - they were most surprised to see a sailor. After being briefed I returned to the beach where we made ourselves at home in the former enemy establishment and set up a signal station after prudently digging a slit trench alongside.

Leaving about 10,000 prisoners behind us, we set off next day for Sollum which had just been taken, and driving a captured lorry in company with an RASC convoy, a boat's ensign flying proudly at a mast we had fixed to the cab, we drove along the main road, which had been built by the Italians, but never finished. We bounced through shell and bomb craters, endured several sandstorms, heavy rain, thunder, reducing visibility to 100 yards and penetrating one's person, clothes, everything; only anti gas goggles saved our eyes. Somehow I managed to lose our leader, and in thinking I was ahead I pressed on overtaking vehicle after vehicle until to my consternation I found we appeared to be leading the entire British army into

Sollum. Once again the wrecked village was completely deserted, but I discovered a hovel near the harbour pier which at least had the distinction of retaining a roof; this we appropriated hoisting the White Ensign and inscribing 'Admiralty House' on the door. Thus I became Naval Officer-in-charge, Sollum.'

AFTER THE FALL OF SOLLUM: AN ITALIAN STATION NOW USED BY BRITISH SAILORS AS A SIGNAL BASE

N·O·I·C· SOLLUM.

The Western Desert Force continued its advance towards Bardia just round the corner, leaving John with his Italian POWs to continue the unloading of supply ships, sometimes as much as 500 tons a day. John describes the Argyll and Sutherland Brigadier commanding a contingent, left behind the advance to picket the place, 'a bizarre figure, kitted out in an Italian Brigadier's tunic topped by his regimental glengarry, who dubbed himself 'King's Harbourmaster' and was of enormous help.' They were without air cover 'except for a few nimble but outdated Gladiators, who engaged in many 'Biggles' type dog-fights with not dissimilar biplanes, CR42s. The port had no ack-ack gun defences except for a few captured Bredas, and on Christmas Eve some 12 unobserved Italian bombers were suddenly right above us, the work of unloading lighters in full swing; there was no escape and five direct hits on the jetty and craft left me surrounded with 25 dead and dying.'

His Admiralty House was used as a meeting place for the Xlll Corps conference with General O'Connor and other Generals and Admirals, and his last job in Army territory was for the Navy: 'acting as a lighthouse for the 2nd Battle Squadron when it made a landfall prior to carrying out an early morning bombardment north of the Bardia-Tobruk road, which immediately preceded the assault on Bardia. I had to find a particular position in the pitch dark and lonely desert, walking by compass course for 60 minutes, when I would find myself overlooking the sea. 'I was to flash a pre-arranged signal with my aldis lamp, at a set time on a seaward bearing for twenty minutes non-stop. This was to provide the flagship with a point of departure for the run in to the bombardment position.

After this assignment I was recalled to normal duty on board a newly repaired HMS *Glasgow*. A Swordfish was sent from Alexandria to fetch me, which I found among the wrecked aircraft at the airfield on the 750 feet high plateau beyond the escarpment. A babyfaced pilot greeted me. 'Are you the pilot?', I asked in astonishment, being more used to snotties in charge of picket boats rather than aeroplanes. 'That's me, Sir', the young man replied, indicating the Fleet Air Arm wings on his ringless sleeve. 'I hope you have your revolver, Sir, as you are our main armament!' Luckily this was not put to trial, and 'in spite of the aircraft's slow speed and vulnerability, and the pilot's (assumed) inexperience, the 300 mile trip was safely completed, keeping virtually at camel height all the way over the desert'.

For this episode, John's local press at home reported that he was being awarded the Distinguished Service Cross 'For courage, skill and devotion to duty off the Libyan coast'.

CHAPTER 12

——— ⚓ ———

THE IMPORTANCE OF WEATHER
AND CATS

For all those crossing the Arctic Circle (70 degrees N), King Neptune awarded a certificate of the Royal and Ancient Order of the Blue Nose. HMS *Oribi*, when engaged in Russian convoy escort duties, crossed it seven times in 1942 and every member of the crew thus earned an extra six endorsements. These Russian convoys of ships, carrying vitally needed war supplies to Murmansk and Archangel were protected by the Allies during the worst possible weather, and throughout the 24 hour winter darkness zone were within easy range of German air, surface and underwater attack for three quarters of their 2000 mile voyage. But if you ask any veteran of these experiences what he remembers, it will always be the weather he most feared. John describes: 'It was rarely safe to venture on deck where you were liable to be washed or slip overboard into the Arctic Sea. Spraying the exposed working areas with scalding water fed from the boiler room froze on impact and made things worse; the rigging, right up to the Crow's nest and guard rails, became ice blocks as thick as a man's arm, and could only be cleared with picks and hammers; the weight of this, if allowed to grow, would cause the ship to heel over to a most dangerous degree. Guns and torpedo tubes were kept operable with electric heating coils, fitted to blank cartridges in their breeches.'

After this, even the Atlantic weather must have been a relief, and *Oribi* was next ordered to join the 3rd Support Group which consisted of Fleet Destroyers. Their job was to be a new conception; a fast mobile force which dashed from one threatened convoy to another, often refuelling at sea.

Their first encounter was in defence of Convoy HX 230 in a SW

gale, when an attack by five U-boats was successfully beaten off with
the loss of one merchant ship. Dashing off to the next convoy with the
rest of the support group, they managed to drive off seven more
U-boats which we re attacking another 57 ship Convoy. John describes;
'We had a brilliant new secret piece of equipment which at this stage of
the war proved its worth....The High Frequency Direction Finding
picked up a strong transmission which its operator identified as a
U-boat meteorological report. In less than an hour it had been
confirmed by the Admiralty, (this would have been the work of Wrens
at Bletchley Park) fixing the position within twenty miles of us; at full
speed ahead we soon sighted two U-boats on the surface recharging
their batteries; after dropping a pattern of depth charges we hurried
back to protect the convoy.'

During one of these actions *Oribi* had picked up 'an oily solitary
figure clinging to a small piece of wreckage', who turned out to be the
badly wounded Captain of a U-boat, the sole survivor. The weather
was appalling, and it was with some difficulty that he was fished out of
the raging sea, at considerable risk to the sailors who went over the side
to secure a line to him, whereupon they found he had a great gash, the
whole length of one arm. John then describes how the Wardroom was
used as hospital theatre for attending to this Korvettankapitan of the
Kriegsmarine: 'Our young Medical Officer, Surgeon Lieutenant John
Smith, a Glasgow gynaecologist in civilian life operated on him. The
lively motion of the ship, travelling at some speed, necessitated lashing
the patient to the dining room table whose polished top was covered in
a tarpaulin; the surgeon was strapped to a deck support stanchion with
a sailor to steady him; to his left the Sick Berth Attendant was wedged
holding the instruments, and from the other side a wardroom steward
stood by to mop his brow. He made a superb job of putting in thirty or
forty of the neatest stitches from wrist to armpit - as neat as any he
might have made when stitching up a young mother after a caesarean
section.' During this time the ship rarely ceased pitching, rolling and
shaking, water constantly washing round the mess decks and cabin flats
while the upper deck was untenable. They had been struck by
equinoctial gales in which the ship suffered severe structural damage
while steaming at high speed into heavy seas. A crack was discovered
extending about one third of the way across what was known in

destroye rs as the 'iron deck' - the toughened steel deck amidships, over the engine room, on which the two quadruple torpedo tubes are secured. As this could easily lead to a broken back, *Oribi* was detached to the nearest port, which as fate decreed, happened to be Belfast.

Although the Admiralty boffins had recently come up with the new secret High Frequency Direction Finder, which had been found extremely valuable when dealing with U-boats, Hitler had a new threat. Not content with magnetic and acoustic mines he now had 'the Gnat', or magnetic and acoustic torpedo, which was also electric homing. A new member of the 3rd Support Group had recently joined - a Polish ship, the *Orkan,* and the four ships had been ordered to the Escort Forces Base at Londonderry to train and exercise counter measures against this new German secret weapon. Sailing orders were on board each ship, already humming with 40,000 horsepower of dormant energy waiting to be unleashed, when there was a hail from the bridge of the Polish ship, 'Our cats have disappeared - have you got them?' Sailors are very superstitious, and this was a serious matter. As it happened, three cats had just been spotted joining *Oribi* moments before, so several Polish sailors were sent over to retrieve them. They managed with great difficulty - the creatures protesting every step of the way - to catch two of them, but the third, with a violent shriek and digging its claws painfully into the Pole, escaped and hid under a gun platform in *Oribi* and from where it refused to come out. All the ships had to refuel from a tanker lying off Moville, and there the *Oribi* found the *Orkan* alongside once more. One of the retrieved pets was found to have escaped again to *Oribi,* via the tanker, so a signal was sent and a boat came over to collect it. Once more the cat growled and fought to remain, but was firmly returned to its rightful home. When *Oribi*'s stowaway cat was coaxed out from under the gun platform it was found to be unadulterated black, which was naturally taken as a particularly good omen for *Oribi.*

Before sailing, any ship destined for seatime would be visited by boats from the Republican side of the river, full of eggs, butter, bacon and other items which found ready buyers; this would be duly noted by enemy agents based on that bank, who would also report to their masters the ships' sailing time and last known course.

John continues the story: 'A few nights later, the destroyers were stationed in line abreast, carrying out a sweep towards a reported U-boat position - I had the Middle Watch and was about to take a sip from a mug of steaming hot cocoa, when there was a distant explosion; in a corner of the bridge the muffled up radio operator, crouched over his tiny blue light, took down a message as it came in. Immediately everyone came to Action Stations, with the Captain already up, summoned by voice pipe from his sea cabin and strident alarm gongs, which roused the watch below. The signal was from *Orkan* reporting the explosion close astern - this signal was to be her last. The very next minute our asdic picked up a hydrophone effect from the torpedo - the Gnat - which on its way to *O r k a n* passed close to and narrowly missed our screws, the beat of which would have set it off - then almost simultaneously, our Polish consort, next in line and less than a mile away, suddenly became a terrible red glow from end to end - she had ignited, her steel hull turned to transparent red glass, revealing violent blazing furnaces below - then the thunderous explosion stunned our horrified ears. As the shattering sound died away the surrounding sea and sky blazed with incandescent fragments fluttering down - a deathly stillness hung about the night. Instantaneously a vast ship, a living pulsating entity, a destroyer identical to our own had vanished leaving a ghostly gap, her two hundred brave men consigned to oblivion, together with her two clairvoyant cats.

The third clairvoyant cat that successfully jumped ship became the *Oribi's* much venerated mascot, closely guarded and pampered by every member of the crew. Panic broke out when she disappeared for several days. It was only when she returned with six matching black kittens that calm was restored and the Fleet once more able to carry out its Naval duties!'

Did they investigate feline farsightedness? Did the Admiralty set up an enquiry into Polish cats' inbuilt occultism? Did they identify animal magnetism? Had the black cat inherited something from the association with witches? Was the acoustic attraction some sort of long purrrr that cats could recognise? Had the cats been indoctrinated by Germans before joining the Polish ship *O r k a n*? I doubt if we shall ever know.

CHAPTER 13

⚓

THE BATTLE OF THE ATLANTIC

Luckily for us, Hitler had refused to heed the sound advice of his Naval Chief, Admiral Donitz, which was to double the number of U-boats and concentrate them in the North Atlantic, blowing up as many of our desperately needed tankers and supply ships on their way to and from England. Hitler liked to think he could command the seas by keeping all his greatest battleships such as *Tirpitz* and *Bismarck* in reserve like huge white elephants, which dared not put to sea because we could match them. Thus, while they lurked in port, their German sailors straining at the leash, we gained the time to build more convoy escorts as fast as possible. Now Hitler had realised his Naval Chief was right, and the Germans were turning out over seventy of these deadly boats every quarter, and by May 1943 it was estimated that 143 were lying in wait for our convoys.

This was probably the climax of the North Atlantic battle, and into all this mayhem sailed the 3rd Support Group, still slightly mesmerised by the lingering effect of lightning romance and the terrible end of their Polish mates.

Oribi left Belfast on 29th April to rejoin the Group which had been ordered to reinforce the escort of ONS 5, a slow convoy of 43 ships bound for North America. Fighting its way through hurricane force winds and mountainous seas, speed was reduced to one knot. Four U-boats were known to be in contact, with many more shadowing the armada. John recounts, 'By May 1st the weather had worsened so much that the ships were virtually stopped and losing formation. Next day a temporary lull found the convoy scattered over thirty miles among iceflows and growlers, but the ships were successfully rounded up just in time for another gale that evening. Thirteen more submarines joined the attack on May 3rd, with many more threatening; twenty four hours later, with the convoy still crawling into the teeth of the gale, Donitz ordered twenty seven boats to form a new patrol line and one of these sighted its van that afternoon. On May 5th forty U-boats were directed against ONS 5 - a Royal Canadian Air Force Catalina sank one of them, damaging another.

Apart from the 3rd Support Group, there were four Flower Class Corvettes acting as escorts of the convoy, *Sunflower, Snowflake, Loosestrife* and *Pink*, as well as *Tay, Vidette* and another Fleet Destroyer, *Offa*. The battle raged: six U-boats sank seven of the convoy ships, *Vidette* damaged U 270, while *Oribi* and *Offa* attacking in succession, drove three more U-boats off. Another three were damaged by other escorts with *Pink* who, protecting the stragglers 30 miles astern, sank U 192. The following day as many as 19 U-boats were in contact, and *Tay* actually sighted seven on the surface at one time charging batteries, and of these, U 638 was sunk by *Loosestrife*. In the small hours of May 6th, we located U 531 by radar and forced her to dive before she was sunk; minutes later we rammed U 125 which was then finished off by *Vidette*.'

This rather terse description, taken from the official communiqué, does not do justice to the fierce fighting of those nights, but John does much better with what he remembers most vividly, not surprisingly the ramming of the U-boat. 'I had been keeping the first watch (2000-2359) during which we heard four explosions as four of our convoy were torpedoed in quick succession. By midnight the weather had turned to mist and things had quietened down. Defence stations was piped, which meant that only fifty per cent of the armament was manned, allowing half of the people to get some much needed rest. I turned in fully clothed in the sick bay below the bridge which I used if a cot was vacant, as this avoided the long and potentially dangerous trip along the exposed upper deck to my cabin. I was abruptly awakened by a terrific crash and a frightful bump. My first thought was that we had been torpedoed, then that the ship had gone aground, as we seemed to ride up over something; I soon realised that this was impossible as we were many miles from land. These thoughts flashed through my head as I scrambled out of the cot, but was quite unable to find the deck. The ship had heeled over so far that what I was trying to stand on turned out to be the normally vertical bulk-head, with the racks of medicine bottles and sick bay utensils. All this only took seconds, and by the time the alarm gongs began clanging I had scaled the two flights of ladders to the bridge. There, I watched incredulously as the ship tried to ride over the submarine we had rammed, and whose conning tower was clinging crazily to our port side. We were in the very centre of the action, and all around, occasionally lit up by a star shell, were Corvettes attacking deadly and daring U-boats, still on the surface, who in turn were trying to get a few more of the convoy before they had to dive. Every now and again would come a 'crump', another explosion, and in the background the incessant 'ping, ping, ping' of the Asdic with frequent 'ping go' as it picked up its target.

From the first report of the impending battle over ONS 5, the Operations room at Belfast Castle, and the plot in particular, became the focus of attention. Signal after signal came in, and the teleprinter buzzed on relentlessly; the waiting for news became unbearable and no-one wanted to go off duty. The build-up was slow to start with, and of course we did not realise what a drama it was to be. The tension grew as *Oribi* was obviously heading for the 'wolf pack' and the plot became a vivid picture of the action, with all of us taking a vicarious part in it. Because we could not get instant commu nication as we would have done today made the progress even more acute. My plotters tried with various spurious excuses to persuade me to change watch, so I might not know of the dangerous drama evolving - as it were - before our very eyes. But of course I could not leave the scene - the days seemed to drag, but at last the Canadian Air Force was within range and the residue of the bitterly defended convoy sailed safely to its destination.

Out of the convoy of 43 ships, 12 had been lost, but of the 40 U-boats involved, 8 were destroyed and 12 damaged. This action had repercussions from that day; and it is recorded that a furious Hitler ordered a decommissioning of all heavy ships in favour of concentrating on the U-boat arm of the Navy. Admiral Raeder resigned and was succeeded by Donitz, the brilliant chief of the submarine service.

I kept the following headline in the paper after this episode, which John alludes to in his memoirs many years later: 'Before me is the yellowing copy of a press cutting which Christian kept for me; from her job on the Atlantic plot she knew *Oribi* was heading for a wolf pack but when things began to get unpleasant, she told me later her friends tried to keep her away with various excuses until the battle was over and we were safely making for Newfoundland.'

HMS Oribi's bow after she had rammed a U-boat

Meanwhile, *Oribi* had assessed her damage. Although it looks in the photograph as if there was a huge chunk missing, only the fore-peak and lower central store were flooded, with the main bulkhead still watertight and the Asdic gear intact. Having somehow shored up the bow, she resumed her station on the screen until detached later in the day to make for St John's Newfoundland. At twelve knots, her maximum safe speed, it took 60 hours to get there. Once in St John's dry dock, the bow was reinforced with concrete, and after a peaceful interlude during which communications were once more restored, the ship sailed down to Boston USA where permanent repairs were carried out.

m.   One Penny

War's biggest U-battle : Navy beats off 25

FOUR SUNK: SIX "LIKELIES"

FOUR U-boats have been destroyed, four very probably destroyed, and two others possibly destroyed in a fight with escort ships of a west-bound Atlantic convoy, announced an Admiralty communiqué last night.

The communiqué said:—

Escort ships of the Royal Navy, in co-operation with aircraft of the Royal Canadian Air Force, have successfully defended a west-bound Atlantic convoy against a series of determined and sustained attacks by a powerful force of U-boats.

The attacks and counter-attacks extended intermittently over eight days and nights.

In the last days of April, a pack of some eight U-boats were concentrated on this convoy. A series of attacks were made, the majority of which were successfully driven off.

On May 1, it started to blow a gale, and this weather lasted for three days. As the weather moderated, further U-boats were concentrated by the enemy, and during May 4, 5, and 6, it is estimated that our escorts were in action with a pack of some 25 U-boats.

The enemy pressed home his assaults by day and by night, in a series of some 30 attacks, and our escorts, in weather which was too heavy for complete air cover, attacked the enemy with determination and success.

Two U-boats were rammed, one by the destroyer H.M.S. Oribi (Lieut.-Commander J. C. A. Ingram, R.N.) and the other by the corvette H.M.S Sunflower (Lieut.-Commander J. Plomer, R.N.).

Another corvette, H.M.S. Snowflake (Lieutenant H. G. Chesterman, R.N.R.) attacked and destroyed a third enemy submarine with depth charges. A fourth U-boat was sunk by the destroyer Vidette (Lieutenant R. Hart, D.S.C., R.N.) with depth charges.

Aircraft of the Royal Canadian Air Force joined in the battle, and carried out many attacks on the U-boats, very probably destroying one and possibly destroying another.

Blown to surface

Meanwhile and almost without pause the escort ships of the R.N. continued to harass the enemy. The corvette Loosestrife (Lieut. H. A. Stonehouse, R.N.R.) attacked a U-boat with depth charges, forcing her to the surface. The sound of a heavy explosion was heard shortly afterwards and the U-boat was not seen again.

Later, further escorts joined the convoy and intensified the attacks on the enemy. The frigate H.M.S. Spey (Commander G. H. Boys-Smith, D.S.O., D.S.C., R.D., R.N.R.) scored two hits with gunfire on the conning-tower of the U-boat, which dived and was further attacked with depth charges.

During daylight hours on May 6 numerous other attacks were delivered against U-boats by the sloop Pelican (Commander G. N. Brewer, R.N.), the cutter Sennen (Lieut.-Commander F. H. Thornton, R.N.R.), the frigate Tay (Lieut.-Commander R. E. Sherwood, R.N.R.), and the corvette Pink (Lieutenant R. Atkinson, D.S.C., R.N.S.)

Towards nightfall the spirited counter-attacks of the escorting force had their effect, and the enemy withdrew. The convoy proceeded on its way without further incident.

First reports state that in the course of these actions four U-boats

➤ BACK PAGE, COL. THREE

➤ FROM PAGE ONE

are known to have been destroyed, four were probably destroyed, and two others were probably destroyed. The convoy suffered some damage, but the majority of the merchantmen reached port in safety.

A Washington report on Tuesday night gave the U-boat sunk in one day of the convoy battle as five—"one with a new secret weapon."

The Admiralty communiqué reveals this as probably the greatest U-boat battle of the war—the figure given in the previous great battle with British naval and air forces in the North Atlantic on St. Patrick's Day was "at least 11."

The original cutting from the Daily Express on the dramatic battle to protect convoy ONS 5, and in which HMS Oribi rammed a U-boat

CHAPTER 14

——— ⚓ ———

DIANA LUCK AT INVERARY

Training courses for Wrens in 1939 were initially in short supply, although they picked up in both variety and volume as the war progressed. Throwing light on one aspect of the difficulties Wrens found in pursuing their chosen careers are some of the letters from Diana Luck whom I mentioned earlier, to her parents, which had been kept in an old trunk and only discovered after her mother died. Diana had been serving in the Wrens in the Motor Transport section, living comfortably at home in Liverpool, where her father was the Bishop, and had been trying by every means to get into the Boats' crew category. At last, when she was sent to Inverary in Scotland, she was expecting to begin her training as a Boating Wren, and it was a huge disappointment when she discovered that HMS *Quebec* at Inverary was the newly chosen Combined Training Centre for Commandos, preparing for D-Day landings, with no facilities for training of Wren boat crews.

The letters do not give an annual date, but I suspect they cover a period from 1943 to 1944. At first I thought they were too repetitive and would be too big a mouthful to swallow, but reading them again, just as they came to me, I still found they conjured up a very good picture of the times. Lack of telephones, rationing of so many things and the general feeling of being abandoned miles from anyone and anywhere are very vividly portrayed - not least the people she describes - so here they are.

Diana writes to her parents on her arrival at Inverary - no date:

'Darling Parents,

I am trying to send a telegram tomorrow but if I can't here is my address. *It's Saturday evening now and I'll start this letter, though I would rather continue it tomorrow when I know more. I am very disappointed in one respect, and that is the fact that there are no boats' crews here at the moment, except one large blonde of the worst type who was a maintenance Wren and did the training with the men in her off duty time and is now a qualified coxswain, for which I rather admire her. However this place has not had boats' crews, therefore there are no facilities for them and no proper issue of clothes as yet, not even lanyards. However, tomorrow or Monday, I will meet the boating officer, who apparently thought that either there were going to be several people coming together or that I was trained....anyway he didn't expect just me untrained. Everyone is most surprised. Isn't it typical? This is a camp of the worst sort - huts and mud walks - bitterly cold and huge piles of coke everywhere. But we have large stoves in the cabins which is marvellous, and plenty of hot water in the bathrooms. The stove in my cabin has chosen to go out today, so it is a bit drab in there, but I am in the next door cabin now. There are about 16 in each room, appalling muddle, but I've bagged two good sized drawers. The place (what I've seen of it) is too lovely for any words, but I'm going backwards as I want to start with the journey. Uneventful - very warm and matey till Glasgow which we reached at 8.30 sharp. As I stepped out of the train, an enormous Chief PO (Petty Officer) bore down on me and said, 'Draft or leave?' and I answered 'Draft - but I'm all right as I have instructions,' and she snorted - literally snorted - and said 'You'll do exactly as I tell you', whereupon she seized upon about six other ratings and proceeded to march us down the platform shouting abuse at us the while. She caught hold of me and said I looked intelligent and put me in charge of the party. The rest of the journey was merely exhausting and astonishingly slow. But after we'd changed at a minute little place called Craig something, right on the water, we joined up with a draft of about 30 Naval ratings from Plymouth, also bound for HMS Quebec (The Combined Ops training base at Inverary). Inverary itself is tiny and attractive, broad streets full of most interesting activities, which I'm sure I shan't be able to tell you about as this letter will be censored.*

It's Sunday now, and I'm finishing this letter before I set out on my walk of exploration, which everyone thinks I'm mad to do. Rather grim having Sunday for one's first day, but this morning we were kept busy by Divisions at 9.30, freezing cold as we aren't allowed to wear over-coats. It's held on the Quarterdeck, a most impressive scene, the entire camp present, (mostly men you see), and the loch stretching away to a group of mountains rather resembling the Helvellyn group. Never having been to squad drill before, I had to be pretty nippy not to do things all wrong, but it was OK and very simple. The Captain inspected us like the King you know, and he stopped and asked me a word or two about boats' crews. He too seemed most surprised that I am to be trained here. Then we marched off to Chapel. Very nice simple service, everyone singing very loudly, all hymns one knew, rather like at Rugby chapel, (where her brothers were at school). *I like a lot of men's voices in unison. Then we had all sorts of things like seeing 1st Officer, receiving Camp rules, seeing Paymaster etc which filled in the time till lunch (veal and peas and apple dumpling). I was ravenous and ate the lot as I'd missed breakfast, preferring my bed to an unnecessary early rising at 8am.*

I am starting work tomorrow which is pleasing, and the Boating Officer is quite unconcerned apparently, as my co-worker has just been in to tell me. I don't mind my double decker. Isn't it funny? Of course the atmosphere is appalling and people seem to walk in and out the whole time, lights out at 11.30 which seems awfully late, and on again before 7, but I expect I shall get completely hardened. Must stop now. I'll write again soon. I'm just off on a long walk, heaven help my shoes. Don't worry about me, I am both amused and interested and beginnings are always difficult, but every hour reveals an improvement or at least a novelty. Much love to you, D

PO Box 2 Inverary
Darling Mum and Dad,
As usual my first letter was one long groan, and as usual the second will be of a different tone. None of the things I grumbled about before are any better, but as soon as one begins to know people, things begin to lose their grim aspect and of course one simply has not got time to think of oneself. My cabin mates are all terribly 'glamour' girls and I was quite prepared to hate the lot, they are always doing their hair and singing awful songs and wagging their hips - you know the type,

but they all kept coming up with cups of tea and bits of toast with baked beans on, and of course, I am as matey as ever now tho' they think I am a bit odd 'cos I don't do things to my face and hair all day long. The extraordinary thing about this place is the 'take it easy' atmosphere. Of course having everything on the spot makes a difference, but people do seem to have an astonishing amount of time off.

Monday was my first working day and Halfpenny (yes, that really is her name - the other boating Wren) said I had better wander down with her at about 9, so I lay and dozed in bed. To my horror, at 8.30 a Wren came in and said I had to report to the Captain's Coxswain at 8.30 on the pier. Nothing doing of course, but believe it or not, 10 minutes later, bed made and all, I was stumbling down to the foreshore, pitch dark, falling over this and that, the whole world seemed to be full of running sailors and the whole loch alight with port and starboard lights. The coxswain wasn't there of course, but we joined up anon and I was told I was to do all the trips on the Captain's launch with the existing crew and just act as a kind of stooge. The Captain lives here in the most fascinating little village about three miles up the loch and

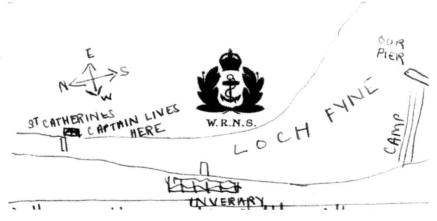

he is fetched about 9 or 9.30 every morning and taken home at about 5 every night. The launch is gorgeous, all tiddley and quite fast. Ford V 8 engine. Captain Ardill is very pukka Navy, and an absolute stickler for etiquette and detail. He has not taken the slightest notice of me, so I thought he was anti Wren and hated the idea of boaters. Well, we got back about 9.30, and then for the rest of that day I just literally hung about in freezing rain; no-one knew what to do about me, there was nothing I could do, and the boating officer was clearly embarrassed by my superfluous presence. The other boater played at being coxswain of the duty boat which runs from the camp pier to the accommodation ship in the middle of the loch, a trip which takes ten minutes; the rest of the time she just screamed and giggled with the men. I was really very angry that day, but enjoyed my trip in the evening taking the Captain home, and all his lovely dogs came to meet him.

Tuesday, I stormed down to the pier preparing to blitz everyone, and the Captain's coxswain said I was to act as bow woman which was terrifying, so I was struck dumb for an hour or so. All went well. Then I had an hour on a duty boat with the Leading Seaman of all the ratings here, who is real tough navy and very dour. The duty boat is an enormous thing like an open lifeboat, so you have to steer standing up and work the tiller with your leg as it's so heavy. We chased about the loch, pouring rain of course, and practised coming alongside, barges, landing craft etc again and again. He didn't say a thing to me at the end, but apparently reported to the Boating officer that I was too good to act as a hand, and in a week or two could take place as a coxswain which is rather pleasing but most unlikely. Nothing doing for me in the afternoon, so I firmly attached myself to the coxswain of the duty boat, the official one I mean, who was doing trips and we actually had a lot of fun, 'cos the Captain wanted to know how the divers were getting on down the loch so we went off to find out. The gale warning was up and we got soaked, marvellous rough passage. By the time I had changed boats (on to the Captain's launch for the evening trip) I was a proper old salt indeed. We dropped the Captain, having gone at a sober speed owing to the sea, and then tore home at 18 knots and it was quite thrilling. Nowhere to dry clothes, so you can imagine the state of the cabin. Then I went to the cinema with the coxswain, just me with all those tough ratings, and the Wrens usually sit in a special place for Wrens only, so they looked v shocked at me, but I had a high old time. 'Tarzan Triumphs', it's great fun going to the flicks here, they all cheer and laugh in the wrong places - you know the sort of thing. Oh, I forgot to say yesterday I went to see 1st Officer as I thought I'd get things straightened out. I said that I really wanted to do the training properly, and even if Halfpenny did call herself a coxswain, she doesn't know half the things a coxswain should know, or would know if she had a proper training. Today has been the most perfect day, the colour is quite amazing. It's all thrilling starting off in the dark, the sunrise, all the boats whizzing about, oh, I can't begin to describe it. I have so many buddies down on the foreshore now, so many little huts I can visit and have cups of tea etc that lack of work doesn't matter; it does really, but not so grim. I go about armed with a huge seaman's Manual. A special buddy is the Pier-Master who has a teeny hut, the size of a lavatory with a huge stove in it; I go and sit there, and he teaches me knots and splices. He is a huge burly 3 badge AB, and has nothing to do all day but make parrots in 3 ply wood and occasionally doll's furniture.

My instructor coxswain (each coxswain I talk about is different you see - I am now talking about the Leading Seaman - pukka Navy) had me out again, I adored it, and this afternoon we sat in a hut and did compass reading and charts etc, but I want to do it all better than that. Got The Times and letters this morning, very welcome. Do write lots, and could you send all the fruit, dried and anything in that line, nuts etc? Food here is not bad but all stodge of course, no veg. I can pinch carrots - the galley (kitchen) girls are horrid here, so you can't get anything out of them. Tons of love darlings, I'll write again soon, Di

Jan 22nd PO Box 2 Inverary
Darling Parents,
I am starting this now because every time I do anything new, I always want to tell someone, and no-one here cares a tuppeny jot what one does, so I have to write it. Tonight I am having an evening, tidying, 'dobying', make and mend, very necessary and I am enjoying myself hugely. The cabin is boiling hot, only one other girl here at the moment. She has a grumbling appendix and is boiling a Christmas pudding on the stove which she intends to share with me anon. The muddle and mess in the cabin is something that would make you gasp, but I can keep myself extraordinarily at home in it, and find I am considered very orderly, though the mess under my bed is as bad as the mess under anyone else's bed.

We had another marvellous trip on Friday, another day of gale warning and torrential rain, snow on all the hills. Nothing much doing all morning. I did splices and things with the pier-master in his little hut, while he painted parrots and talked and talked.

Yesterday another boater turned up from Aultbea full of enthusiasm, to be 'trained', just as I was, but she was rather dashed on learning just what was what. She, Joan something, and I walked into the village to do a spot of shopping. She is so fed up with the place and so miserable that she was the most unsuitable companion, and she did her best to make me down too, but I was feeling most chirpy and refused to be downed. I was rather thrilled with Inverary too. Everyone said how awful it was, and how the shop people were so foul and how one couldn't get anything. Well, I got everything I went in for, although I only wanted a saucepan and some tins of soup and oatcakes, all of which I got and all the people were simply sweet. I shook off the dismal female after a grim tea in stony silence at the Argyll Arms, which she insisted on going to because none of the Wrens ever went there. Actually, the Temperance Hotel is the gay spot I am told, and everyone goes there, and why not if it is good? However, as I say, I dropped her like a hot cake as soon as I'd swallowed my eighth cup of tea (out of a pot, oh joy) and sallied forth on my own. I found a very genial butcher who had some vegetables, which thrilled me of course. I bought some celery and carrots.

All this rain gives one a marvellous schoolgirl complexion. There are two Wren hairdressers here and all service is free. Masses of love, Di

Had a big panic in the cabins as the Captain did his usual Thursday morning rounds, and came into our block (which he never does as a rule) and said it was the most disgraceful mess he'd ever seen in his life, which it is of course, but they don't seem to realise all the maintenance girls need double the amount of clothing, overalls, bell-bottoms etc, to say nothing of always being wet and dirty, and we have no more room than the writers and stewards. We all had to stay and scrub the floors and turn out the whole block, an operation I quite enjoyed as I got warm for the first time. On Sunday after I had posted the letter, I started off on my walk along the road by the loch towards a village called Furnace about 5 miles away. The snow came, the wind blew and it was so cold I could hardly walk. My hands were blocks of ice, but I struggled on and the road got wilder and wilder, up and down through woods, water rushing everywhere, with herons, and gulls and cormorants too, I only saw one hare the whole way. When I got to Furnace I went to a cottage where I knew I could get tea; there I found a typical 'Forces Home' like one reads about in the 'Daily Mirror'. There was only a tiny little parlour, a tiny little dining room, one old woman and about 14 hungry ratings and marines all clamouring for high tea. I dived into the back kitchen, a microscopic room and started to help the good lady, who was a Scotch woman of the best type, by cutting bread, frying on a Primus, eggs and chips, and being general dog's body. She was thrilled, no one had ever helped her before I don't think, and I stayed there for about an hour and a half. How she has all this food I can't think, eggs and ham and margarine galore.

I went to the schoolmaster's hut in the evening and had a very enjoyable evening learning Navigation. I felt incredibly stupid, very sleepy and he kept asking me awful questions, but I was there two and a half hours and it was warm, at least fairly. Today it has rained ceaselessly, does this sound too like a Chekhov play? But I've been out quite a lot as we took the Captain's wife to Inverary pier; that took half an hour so everybody considered that enough work for one morning. I then paddled off to the Schoolmaster to an English class, only me and the sister at Sick-bay were there, but we spent a very pleasant evening over Keats. The funny thing is I have started the cabin off on a quest for adult education, you won't realise how astounding that is until you meet the inhabitants of this cabin; a rougher, tougher lot of hard-bitten young misses you couldn't meet anywhere, and I've got them all saying 'Can I come with you next time, please?' And I've just brought in the list of postal correspondence courses they can take, and they are all poring over them, standing round the fire with their bleached hair in fantastic curlers, and grease all over their faces screaming with delight. Really I feel very old and mature, but aren't they staggering? They've all been here over 18 months, and the Schoolmaster's hut is only 3 huts away from this one. The roughest and toughest of them, one Chloe, is a great buddy of mine and we had a good old hate over the baked beans this evening, and she told me how she had been in the service 3 1/2 years and has been to about 8 different places, and has

Diana Luck

never, never seen anything so bad as this place for lack of convenience, comfort and amenities. I am just repeating this to show that my moans are not completely unjustified. Much as I dislike string pulling, I am rather afraid it will have to be done to get away from here, 'cos for some reason or other, they already have a fairly high opinion of my boating abilities and are perfectly prepared to make use of me as a kind of occasional coxswain of the duty boat. Thank you for all your letters and things, what a difference it makes, we all just live for the mail. I went into Inverary today to pick up my bike off the duty boat which makes an hourly trip to the accommodation ships which are permanently moored in the middle of the loch, about 500 yds away. That is all there is to do. As no ships ever come in here and there is nothing going on in this loch but combined operation personnel crashing about in LCAs (Landing Craft Assault) *you can see for yourself the limitations. There are about 400 men here with nothing to do all day but make and mend.* (Diana's description of all these bored and unoccupied men fits in with the desperate state at that period, when we had hardly any Landing Craft for training purposes, few enough of them at all, even for the operational requirements). *'About 150 Wrens in all, mostly visual signallers, Paymaster's writers, no operational Wrens except switchboard operators. Do ring me up here any evening - do fix an evening and a time (Inverary 23 or 48) and ask for me, I can't ring you. I don't know what to say about your part in assisting my removal from here, couldn't you get to know the Super or something? I should never get a draft to Plymouth Command from here, such a thing is unheard of. My only hope is to go and do a proper training at a training place, preferably Devonport, of course, which is the head of it all and then get a draft from there. There are so many people trying to get away from here that have been here for years, some are really unhappy. This place has been proved over and over again to be a dumping ground for people they don't quite know what to do with. The camp is full of people who have been promised a few months training and they have never managed to get away. They all say it is quite impossible to get away, and you just stay and stay with practically nothing to do all day, nearly everyone is the same and in the end you just get slightly mad and extraordinarily thick in the head. Don't worry about me but please do nose around for me and realise that the longer I stay the more use they will make of me.'*

After this last despairing cry, somehow Diana was transferred to Plymouth. No qualifications were asked for as she had expressed enthusiasm, familiarity with the sea, dinghy sailing, swimming, surfing and a rudimentary knowledge of port and starboard. Her dearest ambition was to be a Coxswain, officially described as 'the helmsman of a ship's boat and the senior member of its crew'.

There's more from Diana in Chapter 21 with 'Twenty Four Hours in the Life of a Boating Wren.'

CHAPTER 15

⚓

WRENS CAN DO ANYTHING

Fanny Hugill (left) and friends who sent me this photograph

As the war continued, the Admiralty found they could depend more and more on Wrens; recruiting accelerated and we were invited to take part in some of the most specialised jobs imaginable, many that would never have been considered possible for girls before the emergency. Another of my friends, Priscilla Hext (Holman), contributes this episode in her life as a Wren Armourer:

'The year 1942 was rushing to its close. I had recently left school for the last time and, with my parents' support, I applied to join the WRNS. Remarkably quickly I was instructed to go to Plymouth for an interview. My mother and I caught a train from Truro and I had soon signed up for the 'duration'.

Christmas was at home and shortly afterwards I was back on Truro station, this time catching a train for Mill Hill in North London, a reception centre for Wrens. It was an enormous school with very large rooms which we had to call cabins, and we were on bunk beds. In an interview I applied to join Boats' Crew, but alas that category was full up. They offered several jobs, but none appealed so they gave me an aptitude test - this was quite fun and I enjoyed doing it. Next day I was sent to see a Lieutenant Commander, Royal Navy, who told me that the test showed I had an engineering aptitude, so would I like to join the Fleet Air Arm as an Armourer? It seemed the best offer so far, so I said 'Yes'. He told me that I would be dealing with guns and bombs on aircraft on training airfields where young sailorswould spend some time befo re being posted to aircraft carriers. Initially I would go for training in Newcastle-under-Lyme in the Potteries in Staffordshire. So a few days later I left behind learning how to salute and march and various other Navy occupations and caught a train with 14 other girls all heading for the same course. We were met by a Navy blue bus which took us to the Wren HQ, where we were told we were going to live in billets in the town. The other girls had all been in the same cabin in Mill Hill and had paired up, so I agreed to take the single billet. We set off again in the bus with a Wren Officer in charge. My hostess was out, so the Officer left a note and I went with two girls who were just down the road. They were shown up to the bedroom, but there was a horrid smell in the room. We had a good search and found it was the double bed; it was wet and smelly and quite unusable. We thought that the baby we had seen downstairs had probably been put in the bed with insufficient nappies. Betty and Pam decided to try and sleep in the two armchairs and complain next day. When my hostess arrived I went back with her to my billet. It was a much smaller house with a kitchen and sitting room downstairs and bathroom with loo upstairs, a tiny room with a cot for the little boy and a bedroom with a double bed. It was obvious that I was to share the bed with Mrs Kay. She told me that her husband was in the Army overseas. In spite of these unusual circumstances, I slept very well and Mrs Kay gave me a very nice supper and a good breakfast too.

When the bus came I was all ready to go, as were Betty and Pam. They had their luggage with them, very sensibly as they had had a very uncomfortable night and hardly slept at all. They needed a better billet very badly, so I said I would not complain too much in case billets were limited. When we got to the Wrenery it was chaos, with lots of girls complaining about their billets, and the Petty Officer who had done the billeting was in tears. I made my complaint, but as I said I did not mind staying where I was for now, although I don't think it was ever recorded.

After lunch, we were taken to where we would be starting our training next morning. We met the three Chief Petty Officers who were to be our teachers, a delightful trio who seemed not a bit put out at the thought of coping with a bunch of girls. They outlined what we would be doing and showed us some Browning guns - and said we would have to strip them and put them together while blindfolded. I think we thought they were joking.

At the weekend I wrote to my parents, and told them where I was (it wasn't secret) and what I was doing as I had not written since I left home. Told them all about Mrs Kay and how I hoped her husband would stay overseas, with lots of exclamation marks!!!

That weekend I started a cold, and it was arctic weather which did not help. In a few days I felt really ill, so Mrs Kay rang the Wrenery from the kiosk down the road. The Navy doctor came and told me to stay in bed; however an ambulance soon turned up and in spite of my arguments carted me off to the Wren sickbay. I was put to bed and the fierce Navy nurse called me Priscilla instead of my surname (Holman). She also asked me if I wanted a cup of tea. The occupants of the other beds all peered out from under their blankets, all bleary-eyed from flu and illness, to see what on earth was going on and why I was being so favoured. I hadn't a clue.

The next thing that happened was that my mother turned up. I think that my greeting was something like 'What are you doing here?' I thought my elder brother in MTBs must have been killed. However, it turned out that my father was deeply concerned at my billeting arrangements and had been ringing the Commander in Chief, Western Approaches, whose office had put him on to the Chief Wren Officer for Western Approaches. She had spoken to the local Captain, Royal Navy, who had laid on his car and Wren driver to greet my mother at the station and had booked her a room at the best hotel Newcastle had to offer. I was amazed and really rather horrified at all this, and even more concerned when my mother said that my father had given my letter to his friend Commander Peter Agnew RN,

MP for Camborne/Falmouth, who was on the night train for London. I was told that Peter later asked a question in the House: 'Were the Lords of the Admiralty aware that Wrens were being billeted where they had to share their landlady's bed, and did they really think this was suitable? Unfortunately I do not know their answer.

The result of all the billeting errors that affected quite a number of girls was that the billeting officer had to face a Court Martial. She admitted that she had not gone upstairs in any of the houses she was supposed to inspect. I cannot remember what happened to her, but she passed out of our lives.

Once out of sickbay and now given a bed in the Wrenery, I had a job to catch up on the gunnery lectures. First we dealt with the Browning 303, learning to strip, clean and put it together again, load its magazine and how it would be set up in the wing of an aircraft. Then it was on to ammunition and the proportion of the different sorts - ordinary, tracer, armour piercing etc to be put in the magazine. We all kept very comprehensive notebooks and sadly, years later, I had mine in my tool box, and an oil can leaked all over it and I threw it away.

We went on to Browning 5s, to Vickers guns, to bombs and detonators, to depth charges and how to set the depth mechanism. It was very comprehensive, but most of us found it fascinating. The three old Chiefies were so patient and helpful, so pleased when you got something right and devastated when wrong.

I enjoyed living in the Wrenery and I made a lot of friends, some of whom I am still in contact with more than sixty years later.

We all passed the exams at the end of the course and everyone was very pleased with us as it had been an experiment to train girls; the antis (of which there were quite a few, we gathered) had to climb down.

There were Fleet Air Arm airfields all over the British Isles, and we supposedly were allowed to choose. In fact, I was the only one who went anywhere near their choice. I chose St Merryn in Cornwall, not far from my home. I have often wondered if I had a mark against my name as one to watch, having a father not afraid of taking on Admirals or even Lords of the Admiralty!!! We shall never know.

St Merryn was a lovely place with lots of very nice people and I enjoyed the work. It wasn't so good in the winter when the cold made life a misery. There were few hangars, so the aircraft mostly lived out on dispersal. To deal with the guns, taking them out or returning them, entailed sitting on the wing with the cold biting through the seat of our trousers and every knuckle at risk as we wrestled with the heavy guns. The Armoury was kept warm though, and had excellent benches to work at. It was all a different place in the summer and a joy to work outside. The pilots were all very appreciative, even when things went wrong and they had a stoppage. They, like the young men we worked with, were in training before going on to aircraft carriers.

It was a happy place with frequent dances and entertainments, and the cinema in Bodmin, which we could get to by train from Padstow, was specially popular as there was a café up the street called 'The Chestnuts' which had an amazing supply of eggs for a high tea. I played a lot of hockey and ran for the Armoury team, but after two years most of my friends had gone and I decided to move too. By this time I was a Leading Wren with an officer recommendation on my CV, though I was still too young for that. There was a vacancy at a place called Eglinton in N Ireland, so I went there. What a journey that was from Padstow to Stranraer in Scotland, by ferry to Larne and then by train again to Eglinton. Luckily I had labelled my luggage as I fell fast asleep, but some woman in my compartment woke me up in time as she had seen the labels.

Eglinton was very different to St Merryn. There I had lived in the Hotel Metropole in Padstow, catching a bus up to the airfield every morning, all very comfortable. Here we lived in a sort of large Nissen hut with rather limited facilities for the number of girls. For work, men and women were separated, each having a smallish Nissen hut but adjacent. I was in charge of the Wrens, but a most objectionable Petty Officer was in charge of the men. He persistently offloaded the worst jobs on us until I rebelled. I kept a very detailed work sheet for both, and armed with this I went and saw the Armoury Officer, but I didn't get much help from him, so I went and saw Commander (Flying). He was most interested in my worksheets, and got his Writer (i.e. Sec) to type it out and then I signed it. He said he would recommend me to be a Petty Officer but 'Paddy' - he was Irish - would still be senior to me. A few weeks later Paddy was moved and peace broke out, and we all worked together and no, I never did get my promotion.

It was a lovely place to work in the summer. There were no hangars and dispersal was very close to Lough Foyle. After work, we would hide our bikes in long grass and nip over the dyke and have a cool refreshing swim - we always carried bathers and a towel in our tool bags. The biggest event while I was there was after VE Day when lots of U-boats came past as we stood on the Dyke on their way to Londonderry. It was a very emotional time.'

When Wren Mary Brown (Bridges) volunteered for a category called 'Maintenance' she had no idea what she was letting herself in for. 'After my initial training at Westfield College in London I was posted to HMS Excellent Portsmouth. I had chosen Maintenance as my category, thinking it sounded fun, but not having a clue as to what I would be required to maintain. It was not until I was sitting with nine other Wrens in a shed on Whale Island that I discovered that Whale Island was a famous Gunnery School. The Gunnery Commander came in to introduce us to Chief Petty Officer Coles, and to tell us that we were to be the first ten Wrens to become QOLCs (Qualified in Ordnance Light Craft). We took copious notes over the next six weeks and learned how to strip, maintain and reassemble all the guns that the MGBs (Motor Gun Boats) and MTBs (Motor Torpedo Boats) carried. These were pistols, rifles, 0.5 machine guns, the Lewis gun, Oerlikon gun and the Pom Pom 6 PDR. It was all quite fascinating and required the great patience of Chief Petty Officer Coles, a kindly person who knew that we had not done anything remotely like this before. On Whale Island all male classes had to double everywhere on the Island, but as a WRNS class we were allowed to march in an orderly fashion.

On passing out, we were posted in twos to different bases. I went to Great Yarmouth HMS *Midge* where for quite a time we were the only QO Wrens working there with about twenty sailors. Our Wren numbers increased as the months went by, each Wren releasing a man to go to sea. It was an exciting life, although hard and greasy work. We were able to go to sea on Gunnery trials, and take a turn in firing some of the guns.

I have many memories of the base at HMS*Midge* and of the little ships that gallantly went out night after night to fight the E-boats, returning sometimes battered, with men injured and their guns covered in seawater, and QOs waiting to remove all guns for cleaning ready for the next nightly foray'.

This account is from another girl who must have been a first:

Monica McConnell (Macmurdo) - a Wren Cine Gun Assessor, writes about the end of her fortnight's training, when there was a Passing Out Inspection.

'To this day', she says, 'I look to see if the flaps of my pockets are outside, because one of mine wasn't, and one Chief Officer, Dixon, who was about 5ft tall, flipped it out as she passed me without the flicker of an eye.

We were then given our drafting instructions. One of the reasons I had been able to get out of the Civil Nursing Reserve to join the WRNS was because I had the equivalent of 'A' Level Maths and I had been told Radio Mechanic was the likely job for me. As it turned out, I was to become a Cine Gun Assessor with the Fleet Air Arm, and so I landed up at RNAS Yeovilton HMS *Heron*, which was the biggest Air Arm training centre. It is worth recording at this stage that Chief Officer WRNS at Yeovilton was the youngest one in the Service. She was Chief Officer Uprichard, and she was slim, beautiful and very efficient. She was engaged to a Captain Hill, and her steward used to recall that he sent her lemons from which she used to strain the juice and use it for her hair.

The job of a Cine Gun Assessor was to judge the pilot's skill by looking at the film of the target as it appeared in the pilot's ring site, and from the position and angle of the target. Then, taking into account various other data, you would tell the budding pilots where they were going wrong and what remedial action they should take.

The young men used to come and sit with us while we assessed their films; we worked in the dark with a small light and you could see their intense faces as they watched the films; they were so youthful and full of enthusiasm. Looking back, I don't think we thought much about their future, and I doubt whether that came into their reckoning at their particular time. Yet they were mostly destined to go out to the Far East where the casualties were enormous.

As I had more advanced maths than the other cine gun assessors,

I was given the task of initiating them into the theoretical aspect of air gunnery. I was only a Wren, so I lectured them with sleeves rolled up so they would not realise my very junior status. However, it seemed to serve the purpose as they were much in awe of me. On one occasion a young subbie asked one of my colleagues; 'What is the name of that Wren who gives us lectures?' to which she replied, 'We call her Auntie' (the reason being that I was about three years older than the rest) to which he replied 'You might - I daren't!' In fact a friend of mine wrote a poem on the subject:

'This way gentlemen, if you please
Sit down, and please don't yawn or sneeze;
The subbies quiver at the knees
Before Auntie'.

The girl who wrote this is now in her eighties, and we still keep in close touch.'

It is almost impossible to believe this next story, but no-one could possibly make it up - and, besides, it has the ring of truth. It is from a very different (and not so happy) Wren Armourer Air Mechanic.

Mary Hilton Jones begins: 'When I volunteered to join the WRNS, I had just left school, having had a strict and sheltered upbringing and my experience of worldly ways was nil. When I told my grandmother what I had done she said, 'I'm so glad darling, every sailor is a perfect gentleman.' These inspiring words were somewhat tempered by the more practical ones from my mother. 'Even if you don't like it you must stick it out as you won't get a ration book if you run away.' So I departed for the initial 3 weeks training on a camp on the shores of Loch Lomond. This was strict, things were done at the double, floors scrubbed and rescrubbed, with regular checks for head lice and learning to tolerate the unpleasant catering arrangements. At the end of three weeks we were officially signed on, and I became Wren No 76132 and was told I would train as Armourer Air Mechanic in the Fleet Air Arm.

This involved a 5 month training at a remote Naval establishment in Staffordshire named HMS *Eagle*. We learned about all the intricacies of various weapons and how to service them, and I enjoyed the ordered routine; it was like being at school. Having completed the course, we were despatched to our Fleet Air Arm stations. Mine was

Donibristle on the shores of the Firth of Forth, a vast complex, with all the hangars and different departments widely dispersed in case of a bombing attack. The WRNS were housed in an old shooting lodge in the hills behind camp, transported by lorry to and from the camp. Unfortunately I damaged my thumb on the journey north and was unable to start work for 10 days, which proved to be the first step down a slippery slope of trouble.

Eventually I got my orders to join Squadron 14 on the parade ground at 8am the following morning, so set off carrying my heavy tool chest, my bell-bottom trousers flapping wetly round my feet. I finally found Squadron 14 and got a very cool reception from RAF Sergeant Robinson, who clearly did not welcome a female in his ranks. The order came to march off and he ungraciously pushed me into a space and off we went, finally arriving at a collection of large packing crates, one of which had Uncle Joe's Snack Shack chalked over the door. We all piled in and I saw by the light of a few candles stuck in bottles that I was the only female in a group of about 20 men, headed by the hostile Sergeant Robinson. I must have seemed like a creature from outer space, with my attempts of polite conversation not made easier by the fact that they spoke unintelligible Glaswegian.

Quite soon, Sergeant R solved the problem of my presence by sending me on a variety of missions designed to fill my day. Sometimes these were genuine, sometimes classic leg pullers, but always accompanied by the threat that if I didn't fulfil the orders there would be **BIG TROUBLE**. It was most exhausting. Hours were spent in trailing after red oil for port lights, bottles to keep mag drops in, matchboxes for air screws (slang for propellers), keys for Davy Jones' Locker and many others, culminating one snowy day in an urgent demand for a 'long weight/wait' I imagined a sort of dock weight and set off, but the weather deteriorated and I decided I would go straight to the main stores rather than take the endless routes ordered by Sergeant R. I knocked on the Commander's door, and he was charming and smiled when I said I'd come for a long weight/wait. After about a quarter of an hour nothing happened, so feeling ominously tearful I asked about the weight/wait, and he said 'You've been sitting here for about a quarter of an hour. I think that's enough don't you?' The humiliation of it all.

I went on leave, feeling rather low, and on my return was summoned by the Chief Wren Officer, a God-like being who became visible only in cases of dire crisis. She handed me a postcard and asked me if I could explain it. My heart sank as I recognised the red ink and bold handwriting of my mother using her standard method of communication when annoyed. She had written, heavily under-lined: 'My daughter is no longer in the same condition as when she left home, what are you going to do about it?' Then, in the primmer old fashioned language of that era, the word 'condition' was a sort of code for pregnancy. This didn't occur to me, but it certainly did to Chief Officer Rumbelow Pierce, who pre-judged the situation without consulting me. She said I must 'tell her all the facts', but drew a blank as there were none, so the Padre was summoned with an equal lack of success. After a long delay the Chief Officer returned, and said I was to be transferred that afternoon to another destination to 'await developments'.

There was no time to say goodbye to friends, and I was worried about my tool box down at Uncle Joe's Snack Shack. We had been warned that the cost of any missing tools would be deducted from our weekly pay of seven shillings and sixpence. A messenger was sent to collect them, and either Sergeant Robinson or my Glaswegian mates had unscrewed the bottom of the box because it was completely empty. I was frantic, as I estimated that I would be in the WRNS for about 25 years paying off my debts. I duly departed and was driven to a grim-looking ex-primary school in Dunfermline. It was a holding depot, a polite name for a Remand House for Wrens awaiting discharge, mostly dishonourable, and indeed they had landed some odd fish in their net. I didn't realise any of this at first, and in my genteel ignorance thought that the removal of our shoes in a sack at night meant they were going to be cleaned. I think I was there for about a month; self preservation was the name of the game. But salvation was at hand in the form of a Wren Officer from my first training place in Stafford, who came to inspect the Holding Depot. She had always been very kind and human.

She walked along the lines of criminals, and stopped when she came to me and asked why I was there. I said I didn't know, and she said she would see me afterwards. She sat me down and asked me if

I was pregnant. I can remember to this day feeling as if something was exploding in my head, suddenly realising what all this was about. I was absolutely devastated, and the shame of it lasted a long time.

Within hours I was transferred to the Signals Department at Rosyth as a trainee coder. It was largely manned by Wrens, the work was interesting and I made wonderful lifelong friends and gradually felt focused again. I still think it was miraculous that I was rescued in the nick of time from discharge (you were automatically dismissed when 4 months pregnant). I cannot bear to imagine my mother's reaction if I had arrived home plus the mythical little stranger and minus the ration book.

My powerful aunt instigated an enquiry into the affair, and was told that due to a 'clerical' error I had been committed to the tender mercies of Sergeant Robinson. It was essentially a job for a man and my name had got on to the wrong list, so I didn't exist as anyone's responsibility for three months. I suspect that he probably did quite well out of it with a new collection of tools and my daily tot of rum as issued to sailors. It was all such a long time ago but remains astonishingly vivid, and certainly propelled me into adulthood with an enduring curiosity and some realisation of what the outside world was like.'

A Wren Classifier, another very technical category, now gives an unusual slant on Wren experiences, which I hadn't come across before:

Catherine Avent, who was a Second Officer Wren, writes: 'I joined the WRNS on 29th July 1942 immediately after graduating with a degree in English from Oxford; I have a vivid memory of that first night in the initial training depot at Mill Hill as we were the first batch of recruits. Knowing no-one, we were roused by the air raid sirens and taken in the dark down to the basement where we waited for the all clear signal to be escorted back to our cabins. Within minutes a quarters officer appeared with a trolley of tea; a simple action which inspired lifelong respect for the way the Navy looks after its personnel.

I had hoped to be a photographer, but there were no vacancies, so I found myself at Marconi's labs at Great Baddow, training to be a Classifier (Linguists and Special Writers became known as Classifiers, and after an 8 week course their duties were connected with the observation of the ionosphere and analysis of Wireless Telegraphy transmissions). We wore 'bunting tosser's crossed flags' (as category badge) and were considered part of naval intelligence. I spent most of the year there working in a little hut three fields away from the building, which meant walking past sleeping cows to get a meal at 3 in the morning when on middle watch. The house we lived in had a stoker to maintain the boilers. Imagine the excitement when one day a signal came ordering 'stokes' to report to the Royal Naval Barracks at Chatham to 'stand trial on a charge of bigamy!' We eyed him suspiciously at mealtimes as he described his wife and kids at Plymouth, and second wife and baby in Malta, from which posting he had been sent home to the UK; only later I realised what a sense of humour the drafting commander had, to post him to an inland Wrenery!

An unfortunate capacity for mimicry led to my being caught by the second officer in charge, who, not unreasonably, punished me with a whole month's confinement to barracks, halfway through my posting to the Officers Training Course came through - so my only distinction in five years' Naval service was to be the only cadet to be sent for officer training while being thus punished!'

CHAPTER 16

⚓

SAILING IN CONVOY

There was a mad rush to volunteer for overseas service as soon as this became possible. If you were selected you would have no choice as to where or when, but would just have to take pot luck and be ready to go at any time.

Margaret Shooter, after the usual preliminaries of basic training, was one of those lucky girls chosen to serve abroad; not surprisingly she had some feelings of apprehension.

'I was given a chit for two weeks leave which was a nice thought. However, after being home three days I received a telegram from the Admiralty ordering me to report to Golden Square (which was an overseas drafting depot) in London W1, within three days.

This was life really beginning; Golden Square was a Hush Hush place. Nobody knew anything and orders had to be obeyed immediately. One had to be ready for anything at any time. Consequently, waiting was agony. After nearly a week we were instructed one morning to have all belongings packed, make no phone calls and be ready to move any time pm.

When dark had descended a coach pulled up, completely blacked out and in we filed. With farewells from the staff and any other Wrens who were not on our draft, off we started to weave across London mysteriously until we arrived at a station with no name. A blacked out train was waiting for us and a lot of other troops of all services, male and female, all bound for who knows where. We started the journey round about 1800 hours, (vague rumours about time), and again we weaved across country going northwards - I think someone recognised the North Star.

It was daylight when we arrived on the dockside at Gourock, Scotland, where was berthed a liner which we learned after boarding was the Union Castle ship *Arundel Castle*. This was to be our home for the next 5/6 weeks, a troopship to travel in convoy. This was beyond my wildest dreams. We were told at the initial meeting and instruction lecture that we were bound for Durban. Other troops were going elsewhere to various destinations.

The voyage was a bit like a cruise, but not as glamorous, and there were a few chores thrown in. We sailed through the Med. Sea, which could have been dangerous, but was quiet until just before Suez. Then excitement started. A message came over the 'tannoy', 'All hands to action stations - passengers report to their emergency points!' Of course we couldn't see anything, but it sounded as if all hell was let loose. This went on for an hour roughly. The result of this was that two ships in our convoy were hit and had to fall out. We understood that we had been attacked by Junkers 87, or 88; whichever it was, it was the first time they had been used. After this, life was very quiet and we went down the Suez Canal. Ours was the first convoy to go that way since the beginning of the war.

After this there was a rush of excitement when we were told that some of us, bound for Durban, would be disembarking at Mombasa, and we later learned that we were going to Colombo. The reason for this sudden change was that the previous draft of Wrens from Durban to Colombo had been torpedoed by the Japs, and all were lost. After this disaster no convoys travelled across the Indian Ocean, it no longer being considered safe.'

Molly Jenkins, Wren Writer, lives not far from me in Cornwall, and wrote this sequence of what happened to her:

'I joined the WRNS on impulse. I was walking down Oxford St in my lunch break and stopped outside the recruiting centre. I went in to enquire and came out having joined up. My boss was not very pleased, but my parents were very supportive. I was 19 at the time and it was 1942.

After my training I was sent to Combined Operations, Richmond Terrace, Whitehall, where I worked for Rear Admiral Landing Craft and Bases (RALB.) When Admiral Mountbatten, Chief of Combined Operations, was appointed Supreme Commander, South

East Asia, we were told that the advance party needed 12 Wrens of different categories to volunteer. Again on impulse I put forward my name, and later that evening I heard from our Wren Officer who came in to say, 'You wanted to go - well you are going - next week, three days embarkation leave.' I then had to get written permission from my parents as I wasn't 21. My parents didn't turn a hair, but I have thought many times since of the thoughtlessness of youth; my brother was in the Army in North Africa, my father in the Home Defence Battalion and stationed away from home, and my mother would be left on her own. When later we heard about the V1 flying bombs (doodlebugs) we were all very worried about our families.

We travelled up to Liverpool by night, and boarded the *Dunnotter Castle* on 12th September 1943 and sailed the next day. We went way out into the Atlantic before the convoy turned south and we ended up in the Bay of Biscay; the September gales were blowing and we were all very sick. We soon recovered as we went through the Straits of Gibraltar and into the Mediterranean, but I well remember the night I lay in my bunk and wondered 'What am I doing here?' But now it was the ship that was ill, and we had to disembark at Port Said. Our little party of 12, plus three WAAF and one Wren Officer had to camp in the desert for the night before going on by train to Ismalia, where we waited for the Lighter to take us to join a ship of the Orient Line, the *Multan*. On this troopship we were the only females.

A month after embarking at Liverpool we arrived in Bombay. We were met by a sign in foot high letters saying QUIT INDIA. What a wonderful welcome! We were under the impression that we were out there to do our best to release men to stop the Japs invading their country.

We went by train to Delhi, which took the best part of a day. Next day I found I was to work for the Army, so it was goodbye Navy for the rest of the war for me. It was Combined Operations HQ with Americans, male and female. I was with Movements and Transportation (Mov and Tn) and I worked for Colonel Bull of the Royal Engineers and we got on well.

There were several tragedies. First, one of the Wrens developed smallpox, although luckily she had been vaccinated so she recovered without having any scars on her face. Then we had a case of typhoid.

But worse was to come, when one of our liveliest and most happy go lucky Wrens died of polio.

In 1944 we moved to Kandi; we flew to Colombo, stopping at Madras en route, then by train to Kandi. From the hot dry heat of Delhi we had to adjust to the hot humid climate of Ceylon; prickly heat and Kandi Cramp instead of Delhi Belly. Our quarters were in huts on the edge of the golf course, 12 to a hut. Pole cats used to run along the rafters, and we blessed our mosquito nets. The HQ was in Botanic Gardens, Peradynia, and our offices in basher huts. After an attack of jaundice I recovered in the sick bay; this was in the middle of Kandi town and was very noisy and smelled of curry. Afterwards, I was lucky to have three weeks sick leave in the hill country of Bandarawella.

Christmas was greatly cheered by a visit from Admiral Mountbatten who came to lunch with us. As Mess Secretary I sat next to him and was worried as to what to talk about - needless to say he kept us all interested and amused. That evening there was the Officers Mess dance, and I was once more 'paralysed' when he asked me to dance. But it was all very relaxed and he told me about his daughter Patricia who was in the WRNS.

I came home in July, a week before the atom bomb ended the war.'

A Wartime Journey is what Philippa Roberts particularly remembers of her service overseas, and it certainly had its moments.

'I joined the WRNS in 1941, and after serving in Milford Haven and Liverpool I applied to go overseas. To my surprise I was sent to South Africa instead of to a war zone!

We Wrens assembled in London, and quite soon boarded a troop train with other service personnel and were given a food package each. The station was dark but for a very few dim lights, and as the train began to move, an air raid siren sounded and I thought, 'Are we going to be bombed now and never reach our destination?' However the train continued in the dark, by I guess a devious route to the Clyde where we boarded a troopship called the *Almanzara*. We departed in convoy at night, and I remember lying in my bunk in the dark when all was quiet, listening to the ship creaking as she slowly rolled from side to side. Quite a comforting sound.

We sailed on down the Atlantic Ocean passing Gibraltar and into the Mediterranean Sea. It wasn't quite 'open' by then (1943) as we were attacked by enemy planes. I could not watch because we were sent down below deck, but we could hear the battle going on and fortunately we were not hit. When we were allowed back up on deck it was clear that the convoy had largely scattered , so we continued in a much smaller one on to Alexandria. In the harbour the natives were waiting in their boats for us, hauling up leather handbags on ropes for us to buy! We looked at these and sent them down again. After disembarking we boarded a train which was standing by the docks; this soon moved off and our journey through the desert terrain to Port Suez began.

On the way the train slowed down and came to a stop in the middle of nowhere. We looked about and saw a small contingent of Army cooks from a nearby transit camp alongside. They were frying dozens of eggs in a large container, which they served on pieces of bread to the whole train! We stood outside in the sunshine enjoying our lovely surprise breakfast which had been perfectly cooked.

At Port Suez a lorry took us, standing all of the journey to another transit camp. It was a warm night, with a full moon shining and we Wrens were delivered to the 'Airary', the nickname for our camp. It was surrounded by a high wire fence and we slept on Italian hospital beds. We were cooked for and waited on by Italian prisoners of war in a marquee. I think they were quite glad to be out of the fighting.

After a few days there in the desert, we were taken back to Port Suez where we boarded another troopship which was the captured German ship *Cap Norte*, renamed *Empire Trooper*. The ship had a Javanese crew and I can visualise now these huge men squatting cross-legged outside our cabins, awaiting our call for a bath to be run. The baths were filled with hot seawater and filled fast and furiously. I was a little scared of these crewmen but they did not do us any harm.

We sailed down the Red Sea, stopping at Aden, a mass of yellowish-brown dust, sand and rock, with not a tree or any green vegetation in sight, continuing down the Indian Ocean to Durban, where we arrived safely and our shipboard romances ended as we went our several ways'.

CHAPTER 17

⚓

ABOARD A MONSTER

I had written a great many letters to promising friends and relations hoping they had exciting Wren stories to jazz up my book. Replies came from all over the place and I ricocheted from them to others; when some of them didn't reply, I was not unduly surprised - so I was particularly delighted when Elizabeth, Duchess of Northumberland wrote - having lost my letter for some time and then come across it - to tell me of her most exciting journeys, and in most diverse modes of travel, which eventually took her even to Australia and right round the world.

She relates: 'I think I was one of the first Wrens to go to sea - and spent three and a half months in the *Mauretania* bringing troops back from America in 1943, ten days crossing the Atlantic and a week in the USA after each crossing.

Thanks to the war, I can say I've been right round the world.' She modestly adds, 'I expect it is now too late to send you my little Wren memories, not that I've anything interesting or amusing to relate'. But the description of her wonderful travels on duty in the communications office at sea as a wartime Wren had whetted my appetite in this tempting way, and I replied immediately and begged her to write me an account of her most unusual experiences.

The Monsters, as I mentioned before, were the converted liners *Queen Mary* and *Queen Elizabeth*, the *Mauretania, Franconia* and *Aquitania*, which had been pressed into wartime service as troopers, challenging the enemy as they dashed across the oceans at top speed, laden with thousands of our precious American and Canadian forces to Britain, to prepare for the onslaught on D-Day. The liners were manned by their peace time crew of merchant seamen, who would not have access to military codes, so here was another wonderful opportunity to make use of the only too willing Wrens to run the signals office.

The *Mauretania* was launched in 1939; it was a name which brought her predecessor, the legendary and eponymous Blue Riband-holder to mind, and shortly after the outbreak of war she was converted into a trooper, armed with 6 inch guns and painted grey. Her gross tonnage was 35,738, she was 772 ft long by 89 ft beam and her service speed was 23 knots. The two *Queens* (approximately 81,000 and 83,000 tons and averaging 26 knots) and the World War I veteran *Aquitania* (45,647 tons and 23 knots) were similarly converted.

RMS Aquitania

The latter was always a favourite of mine with her four splendid funnels and her vast tonnage - she was built in 1914 - at the time the largest liner in the world. Her passenger accommodation was superior to anything seen on the North Atlantic before with a first class drawing room decorated in the Adam style, its walls adorned with prints of English seaports and Royal portraits. The smoking room was modelled on Greenwich Hospital, with oak panelling and beams, while the restaurant was reminiscent of Louis XIV, and the grill room Jacobean. She also had very sumptuous passenger cabins, and became one of the best known Cunard liners. I have already described my satisfaction in plotting these marvellous fast monsters, who sailed across the Atlantic without escorts on carefully planned

RMS Mauretania

zigzag courses. The *Queens*, in addition to a crew of over 1,000, carried sometimes as many as 15,000 troops on each trip, relying on their speed for safety. Dive rsions of route we re not a problem provided the dangers ahead of them could be detected by the Operational Intelligence Centre (OIC) in time, (and they were), and although they crossed and recrossed the Atlantic incessantly between 1942 and D-Day and beyond, they were very rarely sighted and not one was lost.

I waited anxiously for a reply and the Duchess kindly responded by sending me this account: 'Having joined the WRNS in March 1942, I worked as a Coder at Chatham - Area Headquarters in the tunnels. In the summer of 1943 there were rumours that Wrens were now needed at sea in the troop carriers - the big liners known as 'the Monsters', and that the *Mauretania*, an ex-passenger ship, was applying for Wren coders. Our Signal Officer came to tell us this, and I had my name at the top of the page before he stopped talking! Next day I was sent for by our Commanding Officer, who told me that they were about to send me to the Officers' Training Course, and that I would not therefore be eligible for the *Mauretania*. However I pleaded with him and they said they would think about it. I was told the next day that I had won my request! A few weeks later, 3 of us set off for

Liverpool (August Bank Holiday 1943) where we reported to Commander in Chief, Western Approaches. He explained what our lives would be, the duties etc. He then sent for me later on, and told me that my brother's ship was due in Liverpool that evening and that he would give him the message that I was in Liverpool. What a coincidence. He got in touch and I went aboard that evening - and found that his ship HMS *Woodstock* was lying alongside the *Mauretania*! Next day we boarded her, were given our new capbands - 'Cunard White Star' - and shown our cabin for 3. The passengers were mostly British officers going on courses to America.

We sailed that night and went on duty decoding signals, brought to us by the Wireless Operator - we were working Naval watches. Unfortunately one of the girls was terribly seasick all night and we two had to work watch on, watch off. It took us ten days to America, zigzagging across the Atlantic, arriving at night with New York all lit up, and the Statue of Liberty looking wonderful.

We were there for a week and though we did some work on code-books, we were free to go ashore and wander about. The ship's officers, who became our friends, took us out to lunch and dinner in the city. They also insisted that us girls - even though we were only ratings - should be allowed to eat in the officers' dining room.

For the return journey the ship filled up with with American troops - I think about 700 - 800, coming to fight with the British. There was not nearly enough accommodation and they just slept where they could for the 10 days back to Liverpool.

Our next trip was to Boston, Mass. and the last 2 to Halifax, Nova Scotia - where it was getting quite wintry. One of these ships' signals came in from a Naval Escort Group, (which happened to be my brother's) saying they had sighted a U-boat, and a few signals later on they had sunk it!

On returning to Liverpool each time, we had nearly a week's leave. We were only supposed to do 3 trips before being replaced, but one of us had to stay on for another trip to teach the new Wrens - and I was the lucky one!

When my time came to leave the *Mauretania*, the ship's officers gave a farewell party for me in a little pub on the quayside - I left in tears (I loved that ship!).

My only other adventures in the war were my journeys to and from Australia, arriving January 1945 and leaving in December 1945. By this time I had got my commission, (3rd Officer Scott!). The trip took about a month - 10 days by sea to New York in the *Aquitania* - with 10 other Wrens, 4 days by train across America, 10 days waiting in San Francisco for transport across the Pacific. Finally by seaplanes stopping off for 2 nights in Honolulu, 1 night on a small island, 3 nights in the New Hebrides - looked after by Australian bomber pilots and New Zealand fighter pilots! A wonderful journey for someone who had hardly ever left England.

The journey back to England at the end of the year was by sea in the *Aquitania* from Sydney via South Africa, taking four weeks, spending Christmas Day in Cape Town, and invited that night with 3 friends to a party on Table Mountain. We arrived back in England at Southampton in the bleak midwinter, mid January 1946.'

The then Third Officer Scott, now Elizabeth, Duchess of Northumberland, finished her accompanying letter by saying, 'Trying to keep my story as brief as possible I forgot to mention what we actually did in Australia! I was stationed in Melbourne and worked as a Signals Officer in the Royal Naval Headquarters, Melbourne. I happened to be on duty the night and early morning when the signal came through that 'Peace had been declared in Europe'. What a thrill!! But there was only the Signal Officer at that moment to tell it to! I had a very happy time in Australia and arranged to see quite a bit of it with weekend leaves to Sydney, Canberra and Adelaide, even on a trip to a farm in the outback.'

Third Officer Scott, now Elizabeth, Duchess of Northumberland

This sensational career of service in the WRNS with so much exciting sea time and travel must constitute a record - who could imagine that joining up would bring such lucky chances, seized without hesitation and with both hands. One should not however forget the courage which inspired these instant volunteers; they would know very well and be prepared to face what was one of the most deadly periods of that dangerous arena of conflict, the battle of the Atlantic, seething with U-boats whose skilled and determined Captains, equipped with the latest new and ingenious weapons could have lost us the war - and nearly did.

Among a bevy of Wrens who as friends all joined up together in Portsmouth is Phil Murray, who won the Atlantic Star for sailing a record number of voyages as Signals Officer in another of the Monsters, SS *Andes*. Her father was a Surgeon Rear Admiral at HMS *Haslar*, and she started Wren life in 1940 as a Messenger, living at home near

SS Andes

Portsmouth; she describes this occupation as 'very lowly', but instead of being stuck in an office all day as were many other Wrens, she dashed about on foot with important signals from one Royal Naval ship or establishment to another. There

was no uniform at that time but before long she was recommended for a commission and appointed to Flag Officer Submarines (FOS) Headquarters in London. This was during the blitz, so finding her way to go on duty at night in black out London, was not a pleasant memory. While she was there volunteers were called for cypher duties afloat, and volunteering immediately, she was appointed to *Andes*, based at Liverpool.

The *Andes* had been built for the Royal Mail Line and was intended for the South American route and therefore hot weather. She was so brand new she had not even done her maiden voyage. The ship was taken over by the Admiralty and refitted as a trooper, her paintwork being camouflaged in several shades of grey.

There were to be two Wren officers and three Wren coders on board. The coders shared a cabin, worked watches and dealt with the routine signals; the cypher officers also shared a cabin and took it in turns to be on standby duty for any secret signals that had to be deciphered. The radio office received signals by W/T (Wireless Telegraphy).

Phil had never met her opposite number before and they did not take to each other immediately. The girls' cabins were next door and in the bathroom there was only sea water for washing which was rationed to an hour or so each morning and evening.

'My first trip' Phil says 'was to New York; our course was changed frequently to avoid U-boats and each change sent us further and further north towards the Arctic. I was desperately cold (the ship having been built for a tropical climate) and horribly seasick.

When we got to New York we went ashore in uniform, which was compulsory, and to our astonishment were feted everywhere we went and made most welcome. It was amazing having no blackout, and as if the bright lights were not enough we had delicious food as well.

On the westward voyage we carried on board English airmen who were to be trained in America or Canada, British officers of all services taking up appointments in the US, and sometimes families as well. The trooper was 'dry', so we, serving as ships' officers, were very popular because unlike all other passengers we were allowed to buy spirits in the mess. We entertained all our friends and cheered up the voyages with regular parties. The Captain and all the officers and crew were extrememly nice to us and we made many friends.

On several of our voyages we went to Halifax, Nova Scotia - this must have been the coldest place of all, sailing through dreadful pack ice, as if the freezing wind was not enough. One night when we were tied up in Halifax there was a terrible fire in an adjacent warehouse and the ship had be re-berthed in the middle of the night causing us extreme alarm. Luckily the ship was undamaged and we were able to embark our quotient of Canadian troops next day for the return journey, so many in fact were crammed in that a lot of them had to sleep in the alleyways. Because the Monsters went at maximum speed across the Atlantic, which was considered the safest way to avoid the U-boat menace, we zigzagged according to instructions, unescorted, but sometimes as we approached Ireland either north or south about, a fast Naval escort would appear to safeguard our valuable cargo on the last lap into Liverpool.

After a great many trips across the Atlantic, Cape Town was the destination for the next two trips, and as luck would have it, my new cypher companion turned out to be a great friend already - what a bit of luck. The weather was warm and blissful and as there was not a great deal of work to do it was more like a tropical cruise. The *Andes* called at Freetown and we two Wren officers were the only passengers allowed ashore; we were sent to pick up the newly delivered secret cypher books. Imagine the surprise of the local people in darkest Africa at the sight of two Wren officers in tropical uniform! We were met by residents who had been asked to look after us during our visit, which was a lovely surprise. They gave us a very special local lunch and took us miles into the jungle where we were amazed to see local soldiers wearing puttees on their legs but with bare feet! What they were supposed to be doing remains a mystery, but the heat and humidity were about 100 degrees.

The next excitement was crossing the line, (the equator) the chief ceremony of this 'happening' consists mostly of everybody dressing up to court King Neptune and getting ducked as many times as possible. Needless to say, when we considered we had taken full part in the proceedings, we tried to sneak away to get cleaned up for the evening, but we were persued and dragged back to be ducked again, eventually emerging soaking and speechless with laughter. At last, we were allowed to return to our cabins, dripping wet, to do what we could to repair the damage with a very little sea water and to change into our clean whites for dinner.'

Phil married another distinguished Naval surgeon (as her father had been), Peter Burgess, who was chosen to be the first doctor appointed to the Royal Yacht, when she was still under construction.

Angela Mack wrote a book describing her version of life in the Wrens called *Dancing on the Waves, A Wartime Wren at Sea*. She tells of how she achieved her ambition of going to sea in 1944, when volunteers were called for Wren Officers to join the cypher office on board the Monsters. (Wren coders had paved the way, but now the much competed for sea time was for officers only). I have extracted this story from her book, adding a few comments of my own.

There were so many names on the waiting list before hers that Angela feared her turn would never come, but one miraculous day she was ordered to proceed to Liverpool to join *Mauretania*. For days she 'flew about like an ecstatic bluebottle', finally coming to earth at the Flag Officer Western Approaches, where the Duty Officer pointed her in the direction of the enormous liner and introduced her to her colleague, who had been on one voyage already. They were to share a cabin on the Sun Deck, with two fixed bunks, its own shower and a porthole. The decoration and elaborate fittings of the ship made it instantly clear she had been built for comfortable cruising, and there were promising signs such as First Class Only, Bar and Cinema almost everywhere she looked.

The cypher office was in a small cabin next door to the Wireless Room. Here were the powerful transmitters and receivers and all the paraphernalia of a modern warship's communications equipment, fitted with great ingenuity into the space provided where five or sometimes six men would work in watches.

Angela made her number with the Captain, and having discovered they were to sail first thing the next morning, she decided to explore, and barging through the **FIRST CLASS ONLY** signs she inspected the entire ship as far as she dared. There was no work to do and it was all terribly exciting, so she leaned over the side of the ship and avidly watched the comings and goings on board. There was an army contingent escorting German prisoners of war, which she studied closely. One of the officers later told her that there was a Nazi General among them who had expressed the opinion that it was only a matter of months before Hitler's secret weapon would bring the allies to their knees. All that day, men in different uniforms streamed on board, RAF and Fleet Air Arm personnel on their way to Canada and the United States for training courses, some nursing sisters, a King's Messenger and many important looking civilians. Next morning the moment came when all visitors were ordered ashore, the companion way was removed and the humming of the powerful engines accompanied the very gentle movement as the ship glided away from the landing stage, assisted by tugs. The route assigned for the ship's safety took the *Mauretania* far south, and after a few unpleasant Bay of Biscay storms the weather warmed up.

Angela found out that, whatever she had imagined, it was quite a revelation to discover what it meant to sail in a totally blacked out ship and it brought home the possibility of enemy submarines lurking ahead.

After some days of getting used to being at sea, and working in a rather unsteady creaking cabin, it began to feel like summer and sun-bathing began to make the trip more of a luxury cruise. There were cocktail parties every night and the girls were always invited - in this way they were able to appreciate the very grand suites and staterooms allotted to the senior officers, with luxurious bedrooms and bath-rooms, cocktail cabinets, splendid decoration and very comfortable looking armchairs and sofas.

They were accepted as part of the ship's crew with a job to do - they were not passengers; this was a merchant ship, not a Naval vessel, and it was well used to women about the place. They were clearly marked out as crew members by not having to wear life-jackets, which passengers had to do at all times. As Naval personnel they were under the direct charge of the Senior Naval Officer on board, a Gunnery Officer RNVR in charge of various armaments installed on the liner to ward off any sea or air attack. There was regular gunnery practice, when the Lieutenant Commander and his team would test the Oerlikons and then try out the 6 inch guns. During this time, every member of the ship's company not required on deck and all the passengers were ordered below. The tremendous reverberation of the guns was extremely reassuring, a feeling that although this huge ship was built for pleasure she could return fire, and if required with a vengeance.

Anyone who has ever arrived by sea up the Hudson River to New York can never forget it, with the rising sun casting a pink glow over the unbelievable skyscrapers, and the larger than life, never to be forgotten Statue of Liberty.

After a few days exploring New York it was time to board *Mauretania* again, now packed with hundreds of American service-men and a few women. Again, passengers had to wear their life-jackets at all times and remain on deck during daylight hours, and were not allowed to return to their cramped quarters below.

One night on the return voyage, Angela tells us: 'I received a signal during my night watch which, when decoded, said 'To the Captain, *Mauretania*....U-boat in your vicinity 15N by 42W.' This had to be taken up to the bridge immediately. 'I doublechecked and memorised the degrees, locked the cypher office and made my way to the bridge. I asked for the Captain and informed him that I had an urgent signal for him; the Captain at once ordered the ship's company to wear life-jackets and the men went to action stations.

Angela returned to the cypher room to await further signals. She describes how she listened to the steady and comforting noise of the ship's engines. They were really moving, the forward thrust through the water had greatly increased. It was rather too easy to picture the *Mauretania* and the U-boat nearing each other in the lonely Atlantic. 'Luckily a confrontation was avoided and it was years later that I discovered that the warning signal had come from Bletchley Park where so many of my colleagues worked.'

CHAPTER 18

⚓

SPECIAL DUTIES Y AND Z

Only since the 1970s has any account of our Intelligence Information Service been released, and now there are marvellous and thrilling books written by the brilliant and dedicated men and women who worked in total secrecy, and who can tell us what their brains and foresight achieved in this completely silent battle of skills. Their accounts show how ill-equipped we were at the outbreak of war, and how, when we did begin to receive and disperse useful information, there was little confidence that it could be relied upon. We are told how ULTRA was the magic word, the British cover-name from June 1941 for all high-grade signals intelligence, derived not only from Enigma, but from Fish and most hand cyphers. Enigma was the cypher machine used, in various forms, for most signals by the German armed services and several Government departments, and Fish was the Bletchley Park cover-name given to German non-morse traffic enciphered on a machine known at Bletchley Park as 'Tunny' or 'Sturgeon'. Since the need for total secrecy has been relaxed, it is at last possible to explain what an enormous part ULTRA played in our victory, and how many years of war it spared us.

Reading the cliffhanger book called *The Code Breakers - The Inside Story of Bletchley Park* by FB Hinsley and Alan Stripp, one is instantly involved in the life and death struggle the staff of Director Naval Intelligence endured working literally day and night, to break these impossible cryptograms. (I found it amusing to read how in one instance the head of a department had been recruited for his qualification in 'cryptogams', i.e. mosses, ferns etc, as opposed to cryptograms, luckily without any noticeable problems it seems!). The lengths they went to included the capturing of two German trawlers on separate raids, which were kept by the Germans on station in the Iceland-Greenland area for weather reports, and which, when seized, supplied all the secret documents which enabled these brilliant boffins at Bletchley Park to read all important naval keys for the rest of the war, with one exceptionally terrible period, when a new key used by U-boats was unreadable between February and December 1942 - known as the Black Out.

The 'Y' Service category was another deadly secret, never described or advertised because of its work for Naval Intelligence, which consisted of listening to intercepts by various means and passing on the (usually coded) messages to Bletchley Park. Any suitable Wren with linguistic qualifications would be interviewed with this possibility in mind. (Indeed, my sister Anne served as a Sergeant in the WAAF in this capacity, listening in to Luftwaffe pilots.) Until the 1970s, the veil of secrecy remained intact, and like so many of the jobs we did, no-one who had worked in that department ever discussed it.

Here is a selection of accounts from some brave and brilliant girls, who bring alive the part they played in the lethal, mortal battle which involved us all.

Sister Pamela Hussey MBE lived in the Argentine, but the minute war broke out she prepared to travel to England and join the WRNS. She was already a linguist, but took the trouble to become fluent in morse code while waiting for a passage. (Fortunately her ship arrived safely although both the previous ship and the following one were torpedoed and sunk.) She had no guarantee that the Wrens would accept her, as they did not usually take girls from abroad having such a waiting list of eager volunteers at home, but with her enthusiasm and qualifications she was taken on at once. After some initiation into Naval traditions and history, essential Naval maxims, slang and swear words, such as 'cabin' for bedroom, 'tea-boat' for tea time, 'warming the bell', (that is, being early), or 'them what's keen gets fell in previous', (in other words, the keen ones turn up promptly for squad drill), and of course 'Wakey, wakey, rise and shine!' to get you out of bed in the morning, she was sent off to train in London as a Wireless Telegraphist Special Operator, attached to Intelligence, which took five months. At the end of December 1942 Pamela passed her qualification and was appointed to the 'Y' Station high up on the moors behind Scarborough, an underground construction fiercely guarded by Naval Police and dogs. 'The Wrens and naval ratings were taken up by transport from their various billets in the town' says Pamela, the short journey being enlivened by singing such classics as *'She'll be coming round the mountain when she comes,'* *'You're my sunshine, my only sunshine'*, and *'Roll out the barrel'*.

She continues, 'the wireless room was huge, rows of tables with wireless sets and earphones, naval ratings in one half of the room and Wrens in the other, and in the middle a raised dais on which sat a retired Merchant Navy Petty Officer connected to the radar stations all over the British Isles and to Station X, as we knew Bletchley Park then. The watches were 7am to 1pm, 1pm to 11pm, and 11pm to 7am, and days off were precious.

The sets covered different frequencies, the most important being those listening out for U-boat transmissions. Once settled in your seat, and having taken the earphones from your predecessor (and carefully wiped them on your skirt), one placed one's left hand on the dial and started listening, very often through extremely loud background noise. If in trouble, you called the chargehand of the watch, again a retired Merchant Navy seaman, who would suggest 'Have you twiddled your BFO?' The beat frequency oscillator was a small dial to the left of the main dial which could be used to explore round the frequency without departing from it. Your right hand, of course, was poised with a pencil to take down the message when it came. A U-boat signal was immediately recognisable, and remained unchanged throughout the war: (Dah di di di dah (twice). We called it B bar (the morse for B being Dah di di di). As soon as one heard this, one called out 500 kcs (or whatever the frequency was) B bar.' The man on the dais repeated this down his microphone, and the radar stations all swung over to get a bearing. In the meantime, the wireless operator was taking down the signal in groups of four letters - in the case of the U-boats it was very short as they had to come to the surface to send it - which she (or he, if a Naval rating), then placed on top of the set, to be immediately collected by the chargehand and sent off to Station X, where the decoding took place. By this time the man on the dais was calling in the bearings from the radar stations, and these were sent off to the Admiralty by the fastest route available at that time - teleprinter, and to Station X (another name for Bletchley Park.)

I remember once being told by the chargehand, 'New York wants you to check (a certain group of letters)' - the only time I had any response from the powers that were. On another occasion I had completed a ve ry short signal, probably a U-boat, and the ch a rgehand told me that if I did nothing else for the rest of the war I had already made my contribution to the war effort, although I was naturally not told why this was so important. Was it because they were expecting a big U-boat attack in the Atlantic, and this gave them the position? Was it because the message itself was important? Was it that fateful message about the *Bismarck* which gave away her destination? We knew the wo rk was highly secret, and as a Director of our division at the Admiralty said, 'of incalculable value'. I was christened Queen of the Boca (an Internationally known Argentine football team) and loudly cheered as such every time I came on watch. It was enough for us to know that we were engaged in work of vital importance to the war effort, even if it was driving some of us round the bend!

Very soon after the war ended and after 'an amazing three and a half years in the Wrens - a wonderful experience for which I shall always be thankful', Pamela sailed for home in a troopship with other volunteers from Latin America and set about her life work. There, her commitment was 'to tackling poverty and exclusion and to bringing about lasting change'. She was to spend many years among the poor people of El Salvador and earn the MBE in recognition of her work and dedication. Now living in London, a Sister in the Holy Child Order of Nuns, she continues her work under the name *Progressio* - a question of commitment.

Because of the hush-hush work in the 'Y' and 'Z' Service, the personnel - many of them Wrens - all had to sign the Official Secrets Act, so very little of their actual activity has ever been described.

Wren Mary Earl was one of a number of Wren telegraphists and teleprinter operators at Flowerdown, a well-camouflaged Royal Navy radio station near Winchester; manned by ex-Naval signalmen who lived there with their wives.

Mary relates: 'There were eight of us who were sent for 'special duties' in a department called Z. Our job was 'most secret' and in fact we were the only Wren personnel in UK in what was at that time an experiment unit. We were an assorted lot. Six, including one Oxford BA, were university types and two of us were very green - virtually straight from school. Rosemary Vaughan (known as Rome) and I became great friends; we were on watch together and shared a cabin. We worked under two scientists, Mr Bainbridge-Bell and Mr Watson Watt, who together invented the cathode ray tube, which was part of our equipment.

All the very secret operations took place in a long building with the Radio-Telegraphists in the first part, the Teleprinter Operators in the middle and we were at the very far end in a 'Top Secret' area (out of bounds to all others). Here there was a great deal of experimental stuff, a room for developing film and a radio set with a ticker-tape machine and a camera in front of a cathode ray tube, manned by a very highly-skilled Naval 'sparks'. All the radio operators in the building had to scan the radio frequencies, and when anyone discovered an enemy signal, all the other operators were alerted. Our own operator (one of the older married operators) would rapidly tune on to the signal, switch on the apparatus and we were really 'on the job' - which was to identify the vessel by identifying the set and individual operator specifically by the way he operated his morse key.

We eight 'special duty' Wrens worked in four watches - the work was very intensive, and when a big episode came up, which usually happened on the 8 to midnight watch, we often stayed on with the next watch to help. The *Bismarck* episode saw four of us do a 14 hour stretch! We were identifying individual ships or subs by their radio operators and/or radios.

Gradually the Admiralty became more interested in the results and would often phone direct, especially 'when something big was on,' and ask for comparisons with other signals. By late 1940, the decoding machines at Bletchley Park were still struggling to break the German cyphers. All their naval transmitters sounded the same, but in our work we began to show a pattern of identification which took on a new meaning. It became extremely helpful to discover that an individual signal had actually been sent by a certain enemy 'sparks' on the same radio set as .....such and such a signal.

Our results were sent daily to Bletchley Park by dispatch rider to join with all the other enemy cypher messages intercepted by the telegraphists in 'Y'. We felt very proud to think we might have helped to sink the *Bismarck* and 'chase' the *Scharnhorst* and *Gneisenau* up the Channel.

One day, in a whirl of Wavy Navy gold braid, Lieutenant Merlin Theodore Minshall RNVR stormed into our unit, all set to take over his new command - us. His first commitment was to set up 70 ft radio masts - we didn't know we could hammer great support staves into the ground with a maul, but we did. Bainbridge Bell had invented the system and showed us how to use it, but Minshall introduced a new urgency.

He also improved our working conditions (and believe me they needed it), but he had us running after him like lackeys. 'Hey, you there', he said one day, 'you're doing nothing - go and clean my car'. He was a character you'd never forget - one minute infuriatingly rude, and the next a gentleman who would invite us to his elegant home to sit and enjoy classical music with Isolde, his wife. I even used to exercise his bull terrier Clare for him. He had a habit of disappearing for a few days at a time and returning looking a little haggard, and I later discovered about his undercover work in Europe. After the war when the secrecy period was over he wrote a fascinating account of his adventures called *Guilt Edged*, with the story of his escapades, including his time in 'Z'.

On our stand off day, Rome and I sometimes used to hitchhike to a nearby town, and on such a day, 12 April 1941, we decided to go to Aylesbury. We kept a note of our various hitches, and on this occasion they included no less a person than our Lieut Minshall, after that an American lorry, and then a tar lorry (with a rotten driver), and we had hardly started the next when we saw the despatch rider Hack, lying by his Triumph 500 motor cycle at the side of the road. The two DRs Hack and Wren Hyslop took it in turns to take the urgent secret despatches daily to BP. We hastily stopped our driver and leaped out. Hack was 'out cold', a small crowd had gathered and the local policeman was there. Well! It was absolutely vital that our despatches shouldn't fall into anyone's hands. The nature of our work was such that if the Germans had ever discovered it, they could have stopped us with a simple screwdriver adjustment of their sets each day.

We were desperate, so we went straight to the spot and grabbed our bag and told the policeman they were our despatches and headed off into the blue. Why the policeman didn't stop us I will never know, but we made a quick getaway and set off, not to Aylesbury but 80 miles across country to Bletchley Park and with no signposts to show us the way.

I should point out that our pay was very low and we only had five or six shillings each in our pockets. Also we were very conscious of the conspicuous canvas despatch bag, which was too big to be stuffed inside our uniform jackets or stowed in our service gas masks. Travelling to Bletchley Park was by back roads and in time of war all signposts were removed, so Rome, who had been brought up in Weybridge and had a better knowledge of the lie of the land, laid the trail. We had some very odd lifts - one was a farmer with a rather broken down vehicle tied together with binder twine, who asked us 'Are you off for the weekend? I bet you've got your pyjamas in there'. 'Of course, and our toothbrushes', I gaily replied.

With blistered heels - we did a lot of walking - and feeling decidedly weary, we eventually arrived at BP late in the afternoon, and not surprisingly it was very difficult to gain entrance. Our pay books, the despatches etc were taken away and for what seemed a long time we were left in an enormous dining room; we were worn out, very hungry and thirsty, having not dared to stop for more than a couple of scones and a cup of cocoa on the way. Mr Green of the German Naval section turned up with a very welcome cup of tea and told us to take the rest of the weekend off. Sadly, we explained that this would be impossible, as we had to go straight back on duty. Eventually we did get the day off and travel vouchers for the return journey, but had to spend the night in a YWCA hostel for 2/6 each! We discovered later that there was a general alert throughout Britain for 'two women dressed as Wrens, who had 'stolen important documents'. However, we had extremely nice letters of commendation from our own Commanding Officer, Commander Minter, and from the Portsmouth Command Superintendent of Wrens, and later we were given the job of taking some important despatches to the underground premises of the Admiralty, a totally overwhelming experience, which I think may have been a sort of reward.'

Mary adds how she spent 30 years (by now living in New Zealand) trying to forget all she had been involved in, and then 'when time was up and we could talk about what we'd done and how and why, I was invited to speak to the Royal New Zealand Aeronautical Society and had to spend the next three months desperately trying to remember all the details! Funny old world!'

Hope Maclean was another Special Duties (linguist) Wren, who introduces us to 'Freddie's Fairies'. Named as such and trained by Freddie Marshall at Greenwich, there were 400 of them. Hope says 'I was a fairly early entry into the WRNS (March 1941) and a personal friend of Freddie and Elizabeth Marshall. Those who were taught by Freddie at Greenwich had a great respect for him and I feel that later entrants who knew him only as 'Sir' would be glad to know a little more about the beginnings of the 'Fairies'.

Mr LA Marshall (nicknamed Freddie) had joined the London Division of the RNVR as an Ordinary Seaman in 1937. He returned from Denmark, his second home, in August 1939, and because he spoke several languages - including German - he was sent to the Admiralty for intelligence duties. After a brief spell he went to Scarborough, where to begin with the work was routine; but on 16th February 1940 the Petty Officer of the watch brought him a signal for immediate translation. The message was garbled with some words repeated and some missing, and after deep thought, light dawned on Freddie and he realised it was from one Norwegian shore station to another. It read, 'Can you take (wireless) traffic from the *Altmark?*' The *Altmark* was on her way from the South Atlantic to the West Coast of Norway, and was carrying many British prisoners from merchant ships which had been sunk by the *Graf Spee*. There was a stream of traffic in German and Norwegian, some of it from the *Altmark's* Captain to Berlin in plain language. Freddie learned later that for at least an hour there had been no Norwegian-speaking officer at the Admiralty. As he said, 'the ball was at my feet', and he was given immediate promotion from Ordinary Signalman to Signalman.

It was discovered that Germans were using VHF - short range intercommunication between vessels, mainly E-boats, which would carry out attacks on allied shipping using the convoy routes along the south and east coasts of Britain. For intercept units to pick up these signals, the units would need to be located high up, for example on cliffs with a good view out to sea. Freddie was based at Dover to begin with, but after Admirals Ramsay and Somerville came to inspect, it was decided to employ Wren linguists to assist him with the ever growing amount of work. Freddie's Fairies began work at South Foreland, then North Foreland and eventually from Peterhead in Scotland and all down the east and south coasts of England to Wales.

Wrens worked in hotels or large houses, and in some places - such as Portsmouth - even in a van. The one in Portsmouth was on Portsdown Hill, high above the town. By now Freddie was a Sub Lieutenant, and had started up the training course at Greenwich where he taught the Wrens nautical German (and nautical English in many cases!), wireless procedures used by the German Navy, and manipulation of the knobs on the sets. The trainees listened through headphones to messages transmitted by Freddie from a nearby control room, and after two weeks, those who had passed the test were enrolled, signed the Official Secrets Act, and were kitted up, appointed Petty Officers and drafted to Units. As the number of intercept units increased, the traffic from them was not only sent to Bletchley Park but also to Intelligence Centres located next to the Operations Room in the Command Bases at Chatham, Portsmouth and Plymouth, where the information was collated. Many of the intercept units had D/F (Direction Finding) towers linked to them by telephone, in order to obtain a 'fix' on incoming traffic.

Halfway through 1941, Freddie, who had been wearing plain clothes when instructing at Greenwich, was promoted to Sub Lieutenant RNVR, and by the end of that year, the intercept organisation had grown so large that a mansion in Wimbledon was requisitioned and became the RN Training Establishment, Southmead - with Freddie, now Lieutenant Commander RNVR, as Officer in Charge. Both Wrens and Naval ratings' training courses were transferred there from Greenwich.'

Hope Maclean organised a wonderful reunion in London for the Fairies in 2001, but sadly Freddie, who had emigrated to Australia, was not well enough to attend; he sent letters to be read aloud by Hope, and she sent him a list of all those present - everyone had added nostalgic little notes to him - a month later he died.

Coincidentally, after learning about the Fairies from Hope Maclean, two more unusual and unexpected stories with more evidence of Freddie's success appeared out of the blue, having been buried in the attic of a neighbour who had taken an interest in my book.

Joy Hale (Banham) recounts: 'I was hijacked into Special Duties, when I applied to join the Wrens as a coder. In spite of repeatedly reciting my qualifications in algebra and mathematics, the Navy seemed only interested in my knowledge of German, in which I had a distinction at Higher Certificate (A level), and in which I had become fluent while staying with a German family. I was sent to do a German test at the Admiralty, but no-one explained why. When my call-up papers came, my category was stated to be Special Duties (L), which meant nothing to me.

So, on 1st February 1942 I set off to war. Our general training was curtailed because of a shortage of instructors, so I never learnt much about squad drill and missed the lecture on 'Sex and Society' which I might have found useful. Twelve of us made our way to Southmead, the training and drafting depot of the Special Duties category. This was a big Edwardian mansion, complete with ballroom and neglected grounds, situated between Wimbledon and Southfields and commanded by the formidable (by now) Lt Cdr Freddie Marshall. Both men (mainly Jewish refugees) and women (mostly well-educated daughters of middle class families) were trained there; the men lived in, and we were billeted in an ordinary family house nearby where the washing facilities were speculative; 'I was lucky to meet a lady at church, who gave me a standing invitation to tea and a bath.

It was on my arrival at Southmead that I first learned what Special Duties was all about. I was told, 'You listen to German ships talking to each other and write down what they say'. I was somewhat taken aback, as nothing had prepared me for this and I was not confident that I could do it. Moreover I felt slightly intimidated by the company in which I found myself. I was eighteen and straight from a country grammar school, with a strict nonconformist background, and here I was competing with such people as Dawn Thompson, who had just come back from studying singing in the Conservatory at

Lisbon, Ann Turner, who had led a sophisticated life in London and several others with confident, bossy manners and far more experience of the world than myself. Only Hilda Frestone seemed to be on a par with me and we became good friends.

I applied myself to the training and soon discovered if you knew what the ships were likely to be saying, it was easier to hear what they said, and also there was a sort of speechwriting method for writing it all down, so it was not really as daunting as I had feared. At the end of the three week course Hilda and I found we had passed, whereas Ann Turner and friends had failed and had to do the course again. In the meantime we were kitted, rated up to Acting Petty Officer and asked which stations we would like to go to.

I was sent to Coverack where I quickly learned that training is one thing, but real life is quite different. What we had been taught was mainly the sort of radio communications that took place between E-boats on VHF (Very High Frequency), and no mention had been made of monitoring fixed stations on H/F. At Coverack we watched the lighthouses on the Brest peninsular, who talked to each other in Q-code and sent their messages in the three-letter Harbour Defence code. This took me completely by surprise, but with the help of the other operators I soon learned to handle it.

Also while at Coverack I learned the art of D/F (Direction /Finding), which before radar was the only means of determining where a signal was coming from. Most stations had a specially built separate wooden tower building for this, but at Coverack the aparatus consisted of an H-dipole (a kind of aerial), mounted on the roof and attached to a long pole which came down into the watchroom. The pole was turned by a car steering wheel, with a painter attached, which gave a reading on a band, divided into 360 degrees and zeroed on North. On detecting your signal, you swung the wheel back and forth until you found the point where the signal faded right out, and that was your reading. If two stations could get a bearing on the same signal, or better still three, you got a fix which could be very useful to our Coastal Forces.'

Having gained considerable experience at St David's, near Haverfordwest and then on the Kent coast, Joy decided to try for promotion to Chief Petty Officer. 'To do this we had first to learn, by

130

our own efforts, to read morse at 15 words per minute, and then do a six week course at Southmead.' After some problems in finding people to help her practise, she achieved the required speed. 'So, in January 1943 I went back to Southmead for the course, which I thoroughly enjoyed. In addition to improving our morse speed still further up to about 25 w.p. m ., we also learned the highly disciplined procedures used by the major German naval wireless stations - and the U-boats. It was fascinating stuff. The operators on the big stations sent beautiful morse and although the U-boats did not often break radio silence, it was quite exciting when one came up.

At the end of the course those of us who passed were rated Chief Petty Officer. This was a rank of enormous prestige. On the rare occasions when I went into the ports, young sailors would nudge each other, and say, 'Coo, look, a Chief Sparker!', giving me, no doubt, the same respect accorded to the grizzled old veteran chiefs they had met in the signal schools, and I was not yet 21!

When the course ended we were asked where we would like to go. Having been born and brought up in Norfolk I said 'Anywhere except Norfolk', as I wanted to see more of the world. So they sent me to Sheringham, some thirty miles from my home where I remained for thirteen months! I was very happy there and among the girls I met was Biddy Crudys (now Pledge), who has remained a friend for life.

Sheringham was a small but busy station in the charge of Second Officer, Elizabeth Marshall, wife of the famous Freddy. The quarters were in a big house on the cliff's edge, and the watchroom, half of which was occupied by WAAF intercept operators, stood on Beeston Hump, the highest piece of cliff in the neighbourhood. There was plenty of E-boat traffic, as both convoy routes passed within visual range. It was here that for the first time I saw the whole intercept operation come together. We picked up E-boat signals and identified the boats; together with Trimingham and Hamsby, where the signals were also audible, we got a fix on them and quickly telephoned the information to the Intelligence Centre in Chatham. Chatham notified Coastal Forces at Lowestoft and Yarmouth, who sent their MTBs and MGBs racing up to the spot. A short time later we heard gunfire, and going out on to the cliffs, we saw the flashes of the 'dust up' going on about four miles out. From the signals which followed, it appeared that the E-boats had been seen off without completing their mission, which had been to place mines along the inner lane. This was a textbook operation, but it was only occasionally that everything worked out so precisely.'

Joy had a most varied career, being frequently sent to help out with her valuable qualifications and operational experience. At one time she was very much in the firing line, halfway between Folkestone and Dover, with German guns shelling from time to time. She saw the first V1 doodlebug that came over and blew up in a field further inland. 'After that', she says, 'they were a frequent feature in the sky and we would watch our fighters go up and try to tip their wings so that they turned round and went back again.

After D-Day, and as the Allied advance continued, the German naval stations were over-run one by one, and closed down with such dramatic messages as 'Auf Wiedersehen für immer', 'Auf Wiedersehen Erwigkeit', and even the odd defiant 'Heil Hitler!' We heard Admiral Raeder announce Hitler's death, there was some solemn Wagnerian music and then silence.

This was the end of the active phase of Special Duties, though not of my Naval career. I went on to translate captured German documents at Chelsea, to my OTC at Greenwich, to Germany where I helped to de-Nazify Hamburg, and eventually to civilian life, to the Women's Royal Naval Volunteer (Wireless) Reserve, where I taught morse to young Reservists.'

Now comes the second long lost gem found in my friend's attic which describes what happened to another of 'Freddie's Fairies'.

Daphne Baker (Humphrys) started the war as a VAD in Canterbury Hospital. Driven there at 6am by her father's chauffeur driven car, she spent her days scrubbing and emptying bedpans, until being fetched once more and taken home in time to change for dinner. The promise of being allowed to attend a surgical operation forced her to face the fact that almost any other war work would be preferable. 'Then' Daphne tells us, 'I heard that the WRNS were recruiting in Dover and as I'd always hero-worshipped the Navy, I went straight there, was given a lovely welcome and signed on. By the end of September 1939 I was a Coder in the Casemates at Dover, working alongside the sailors we were to replace, who gallantly treated us as welcome equals. After a few weeks I was sent, still in civilian clothes, to the second ever OTC course at Greenwich. I was lucky enough to be sent straight back to Casemates as a Cypher Officer, sharing a tiny dorm in the tiny Wrenery on Marine Parade, with just the road between us and the harbour. I have to say that the phoney war was enormous fun. I loved the work and the friendships and being able to see old friends on leave, and occasionally my parents 10 miles away at Bishopsbourne. Then suddenly there was Dunkirk, and Dover became the focus of the evacuation - the signals piled up so we could only deal with Most Immediate. With difficulty we got per mission to work night watches to try to cope. Almost every brass hat in the country was working and sleeping in the Casemates to back up our own Vice Admiral, Dover, Sir Bertie Ramsay, and we had to pick our way through their sleeping bodies to deliver the signals. The harbour was so crammed with vessels of all sizes that you couldn't have dropped a pebble between them, let alone a bomb.

If we had time off during the day we used to go down to the quay to meet the troops coming off the boats, and send off letters and messages to their families for them. I think I expected them to be overjoyed to be home, but they walked like automatons, too tired for any emotion. They didn't know then that what looked like defeat would pass into the English language as a refusal to be defeated.

Among all the losses a nice thing happened. We were on night watch and reports of sinkings were pouring in, including the ship of the husband of a fellow cypher officer. We whisked the signal away so that she couldn't see it, but were heartbroken for her. Early in the morning there was a sudden scuffle and a figure in a blue French smock burst into the cypher office and clasped this girl to his bosom. I don't know how many times he had been sunk and picked up that night, but there was her husband and one happy ending.

After Dunkirk there were a few halcyon days with the pressure off, and we could swim in the harbour. I must have gone out rather far because on swimming back I realised that troops were laying double rolls of barbed wire along the beach. With a shout of 'Oi, wait for me', I scrambled out of the water and was let through with appropriate jokes from us all about finishing the war on 'the right side.'

Daphne's fate in the Wrens was completely changed one day when she was languishing in the Wrenery with an ear infection, and the Chief Officer came in looking worried and asked if anyone could speak German. Daphne admitted that she could 'a bit'. She explained that she had spent six months with a charming 'German without tears' family in Munich, studying German and music, having one to one lessons, but mostly social conversation. She had also done a secretarial course as her father, who was then ambassador in Baghdad, wanted her to act as his Hon Attachee.

She was a natural for Freddie's Fairies, and without further discussion she was sent to the Admiralty, where her interview went: 'Sprechen sie Deutsch?'. 'Ja'. 'Do you do *The Times* crossword?'. 'Yes'. 'You're in', they said. And she was.

'My orders', she says, 'were to proceed to an empty Trinity House

Daphne Baker (Humphrys)

cottage on the South Foreland cliff, (South Foreland is the nearest point in Britain to France, then German occupied), where I would be joined by two German speaking Chief Petty Officers as well as a couple of radio operators from Flowerdown, with a van and VHF sets. Our job was to find out whether the German vessels in the Channel were using R / T, and if so, to establish which frequencies they were using and intercept the signals.

This was all Top Secret, and for even mentioning VHF, now a household word, I could be shot and I still feel guilty saying it. We were also to be out of uniform and our unbelievable cover was that we were factory girls on holiday. Coming back in the train I remember thinking the only way to keep a secret is not letting anyone know there's a secret to keep. (Difficult when you are bubbling with excitement). I'd been very put off by pompous officers at parties saying 'Don't ask me what I do,' implying that they were supremely hush hush. I didn't really want to leave my

134

friends and work in Dover, but none of us would ever forget our total willingness to do anything in or out of our power to serve, aroused by Churchill's speeches and leadership after Dunkirk.

So, within 24 hours there we were on the cliff. The green van, with its telltale VHF and DF aerials, and VHF sets was there, parked alongside the three cottages. Freddie Marshall was with us off and on to explain, encourage and help us. I had only recently discovered that the whole thing was his original idea, and for such a young man to have pushed it through to the top says everything for him.

The Charge-hand from Flowerdown and his mate showed us how to work the sets, and which bands we were to cover and search. The first thing we picked up was a flood of plain language R / T (Radio Telephony) from the German Army as it moved through France from village to village towards the coast. The naval transmissions from E-boats or destroyers we were looking for were only expected at night, any movement in the Channel being visible from both sides, so our real job was from dusk to dawn, endlessly sweeping the specified band, pausing on any carrier wave to see if it would turn into a signal, and then on again. I did wonder about this working 12 hours every night, and after about 6 weeks, went to see my Chief Officer to ask how long I was supposed to do it. She said, 'For the duration, Humphrys', which seemed at that time a reasonable request, so I saluted and left.

After a night's work, head buzzing from the earphones, I had to write a report to the Admiralty. My orders were to send this by registered post from the village post office nearly two miles away. We used to walk in, having no transport, and the lady behind the counter would copy out the address, saying 'DSD9 dear? The Admiralty? Is that right?', thus totally blowing our factory girl image. I loved these paradoxes. Just as well, as like many a young officer in charge, I found I was responsible for my crew's welfare, including their pay. To get this, I had to walk to the far side of the village in my cotton dress with my uniform in a bag and change behind the hedge, catch the bus into Dover, find the pay office, which was on the far side of the harbour, and then do it all in reverse.

Our system of communication took a step up from the walk to the post office, when it became the duty of a Naval Despatch Rider to come and collect our daily report. After a long night I had as usual translated the signals and tried to make sense of it for the report, when I was told, over the telephone, that it was too dangerous for the DR to come over, because of the shelling. I looked at our tired drawn faces and thought if the report doesn't go in, it makes nonsense of all our work. So I got in the van and drove it myself, choosing the narrow coast road as being slightly shorter than the 5 mile main road. The Chief of Staff in Dover Castle took the report and said 'Thank you', without even looking up - so I sleepwalked out again.

Meanwhile our masters at the Admiralty must have thought we were worth investing in, because we were moved first into the old South Foreland Lighthouse, abandoned because the cliff had fallen away, and then into the windmill about 100 yards behind it. There at last we had a proper watch room, twice as many sets, three times as many CPOs and the van still alongside for D/F bearings. The windows of the windmill faced right across the Channel, and in those early days it was terrible to see our ships being sunk by Stukas, right in front of us. We were stuck to our sets listening on the aircraft frequencies, and I was relieved to see that mine was not the only hand that was shaking as we wrote.

Another time, we were concentrating on an aircraft, call sign HABICHT, spotting for the German Cross-Channel guns, when a shell fell into the sea just below our windmill; the spray came up to the top of the cliff and we heard the spotter say in German, 'Just a bit further and you've got the windmill!' Our scribbling stopped dead and we looked at each other, and I said, 'We had better get under the table', which we did, feeling a bit silly.

By now the shelling had started in earnest, and for several reasons we came in for a lot of it. Firstly because a lighthouse and a windmill make a good practise target, even if the Germans did not know we were there. Secondly, if Dover Harbour was being bombed, ships would scurry out as close under our cliff as possible, and thirdly, because our own cross-Channel guns, Winnie and Pooh, were less than a mile behind us. These were under the command of the Royal Marine Commandos, who became our greatest allies, sending their doctor if any of us was ill, and warning us when they were going to fire, as we had to open all our windows. They also gave wonderful parties for us at their Mess in the village and we were heartbroken to hear how many of them never came back from the Dieppe raid.

Having no diary I can't remember when the Commando Doctor insisted on my going on a week's leave - only to discover that I had lost the ability to sleep. You can use willpower to stay awake, but not to go to sleep. It was my only war wound.

In the summer of 1941 we had an official visit from our much loved Admiral Sir Bertie Ramsay. After inspecting everything, apparently with favour, he said, 'You know I can't leave you here.' I said 'But we are very happy, Sir, and would rather be here than anywhere.' He said 'But what am I going to say to your fathers?' So the station was moved and my new job was back in the Casemates, Dover, to correlate all 'Y' information in the area.'

Intermingled with this exciting account of Daphne's war, she says, 'May I say that the whole of my service in Y was irradiated by the fact that I met the love of my life on June 20th 1940, the only date I don't need a diary for.' It happened that her home, 10 miles inland from Dover had been taken over by the Army, and her mother was allowed to stay on, in part of it. When a friend wrote to her mother asking her to be kind to her gunner son, she wrote back, 'I can't be kind to anyone. I'm occupied. But I have a daughter in Dover. Tell him to ring her up.'

Alfred Baker

Daphne says, 'So Alfred Baker and I met on a blind date at the 2 mile limit from South Foreland. A few days later coming off watch, I saw the Eastern Arm at Dover - where he was stationed - being systematically dive bombed, and shed a tear. But he survived, and from then on we spent every rare moment off duty together.

And in August 1941, after leaving South Foreland for the last time to go on leave, 'My sadness was forgotten in getting engaged to Alfred'.

CHAPTER 19

⚓

BLETCHLEY PARK

As well as 'Y' and 'Z' units in the Naval Intelligence Service, there was Bletchley Park, or Station X, itself - always surrounded by a mysterious and impressive aura - and where a large number of Wrens worked alongside civilians.

*The brilliant
Alan Turing*

The Wrens played a valuable part in at least one particular aspect of this organisation. Alan Turing, the especially brilliant mathematician, had constructed a mechanical precursor of the modern electronic computer to speed up the mathematical calculations performed by the cryptanalysts, and in Patrick Beesly's book *Very Special Intelligence*, he describes how. 'There were dozens of these ponderous machines, some at Bletchley Park, others as far apart as Eastcote and Stanmore, which employed some 1200 Wrens who tended these monsters. Why only Wrens were chosen for this monotonous work is not clear. It was a soul-destroying job and very like being in prison, except there was no remission for good conduct. Quite the reverse: once detailed, that remained the lot of these devoted and highly intelligent girls for the duration. There were few chances of promotion, no contact with the rest of the Navy and due to the very necessary security restrictions, little social life when off duty. Mechanical servicing of these 'bombes', as they were known, was the responsibility of a small band of RAF technicians, whose life was no more interesting than that of the Wrens. Almost the only recognition that this dedicated band of men

A Wren operates a mock-up of Turing's Bombe – one of thousands of exhibits on view at Bletchley Park.

and women received was a typical message, greatly appreciated from Winston Churchill commending them for the fact that 'the chickens were laying so well without clucking' - Winston made this comment several times it seems.'

The following accounts more than illustrate Patrick Beesly's description, and a most apposite story comes from one of the very girls involved.

Sheila M Carman recalls what she did in *Memoirs of a Wren 1943-1946*.

'In November 1943 I joined the WRNS, my first posting being to a large boys' school in Mill Hill, the boys having been evacuated to the countryside. We spent hours practising marching and to this day I can march forwards, about turn and right and left incline. Our heads were examined for nits, and our nether regions for goodness knows what and eventually we were issued with uniforms.

Next we had to be slotted into a category, and at that time the only ones open were the kitchens or SDX, Special Duties X, which was so secret no-one could tell us what it was. So most of us agreed to the latter, signed the Secrets Act and were posted to our various stations for training in our duties. I was sent to Eastcote in Middlesex.

SDX turned out to be the breaking of the German code. Messages from the enemy were intercepted and transmitted to a large manorhouse called Bletchley Park in the county of Buckinghamshire. There the brains of the country were gathered; learned professors and clever crossword puzzle solvers, who apparently make good code breakers. By 1942 a faster result was needed, and it was decided to use machines for which Wrens were specially recruited.

The machines were called 'bombes' and were about 7' high and 7' wide. We received from Bletchley Park a 'plan' or menu that looked a bit like a map, and according to that, one fitted large metal drums on to sprockets on the front of the machines, about 30 in all, and went round the back to push in plugs, rather like an oldfashioned telephone switchboard. Then the machines were switched on and the drums revolved and went through every permutation on those particular settings. When the machine came to a halt, you read off the numbers from the side of the bombe and they were relayed to Bletchley Park. You were always told when you had broken the code, although not the contents of the message. The work went on non-stop so we worked in shifts throughout the day and night, weekends and public holidays.

After a while we were posted to a station out in the countryside, a large house called Gayhurst Manor. There were about four Wreneries a few miles apart, but in a rough circle round Bletchley Park. There was no transport laid on for us, so if and when you had leave you had to go to the end of the lane and hitch a ride. Private cars hardly ever stopped, but the lorry drivers were marvellous. Perhaps the sight of a Wren in her tight navy blue skirt trying to clamber on to the first very high step into the cab was somewhat intriguing.

When on the 8pm to 2am shift we took it in turns to cook a light supper for the rest of the watch of about 10 girls. Once when my friend and I were the cooks, all the electricity failed, so there were no lights or cooking facilities and we had to try to cook Welsh Rarebit in the boiler house, by opening the door of the huge boiler and resting the toast on a makeshift rack.

About 50 years later, while I was visiting a godchild in Washington, USA, I was taken to a museum of cryptology and introduced to the curator as having worked on bombes in England during the war.

While going on a tour of the museum, our group was joined by an American who said he was thrilled to meet me as he had designed the first American bombe, which was in the museum, and I was the only English woman he had ever met who had worked on them. He also said how fortunate we were that the Germans had no idea of the work going on, or we would have been annihilated. And there we were feeling so safe in the wilds of Buckinghamshire.'

Another brief account comes from Graeme Laing who went to the Naval Establishment P 5 at Eastcote. Graeme gives much the same story, although she joined the WRNS straight from school at seventeen and a half, and was more mesmerised by the strange and secret work than afflicted by the monotony. 'We knew that the machines we operated were breaking German codes and that secrecy was of paramount importance, but no actual skill was required in the work that we did. We worked in pairs and were given a 'menu' from which we 'plugged up' the back of the machine with a plethora of electrical wiring. That done, the machine was switched on and several banks of drums revolved on the front. Every now and then the machine would stop, and the operating Wren would read off the drums a series of letters which would be forwarded to Bletchley Park. Each 'stop' gave a potentially code breaking combination, but in point of fact only a small number of such 'stops' actually broke a code. When the machine you were personally operating produced such a 'stop', word would come back from Bletchley and an announcement came over the Tannoy (loudspeaker) system that Wren Whomsoever's 'Job had come up', and everyone cheered and clapped and you felt like a hero though you had done nothing more than operate the machine as required.

The machines were maintained by RAF technicians, which gave plenty of scope for romance, though there were those who felt that an injection of talent from the Brigade of Guards would not come amiss.

The workforce was divided into 3 'watches' consisting of about 80 girls in each, and performing rather like 'Houses' at school. All the members of a Watch lived in the same Nissen huts, worked, ate and went off duty together. There was a good deal of healthy inter-watch competition and we were all convinced that our particular watch was the best. Work time was divided into three watches so the machines never stopped, and we never slept at the same time for more than ten days at a time, which was quite hard on the system.

At the end of each period we had four days Stand Off leave, and scattered to our various homes, to social whirls in London (the Lansdowne Club was a great gathering place) or to stay with friends and relations.

Looking back on it all, I think quite the most remarkable thing was that the secrecy remained absolute. We were, after all, a very ordinary bunch of girls from all walks of life. We had best friends outside the WRNS, we had interested and concerned families, some of us got drunk or may have been tempted to show off, some of us might just have been careless - but against all the odds, the Enigma secret remained intact until long after the war.

The highly secret Enigma machine

I have so many marvellous and memorable vignettes which are surely shared by my P 5 contemporaries: dancing round the work-bays to *Music While you Work*, climbing out of windows to go on illegal sprees, fried spam in the British Restaurant in Eastcote (oh, so good!), flying bombs (not so good), mounds of greasy margarine on tables in the canteen, polishing the cabin's floors with Lord Nuffield's Gift to Servicewomen - free STs! (sanitary towels!), but most of all the good companionship and the lasting friendships that we formed, many of which have lasted through the years of our very different lives'.

An article in the *Daily Telegraph* triggered a letter from Stan Ingram from which I quote:

'Sir, The report 'Bletchley hums again to the Turing bombe' (September 7th 2006) took me back more than 60 years to the smell of hot machinery and constant noise. As a young RAF technician, I worked at Bletchley Park and its outstations over a number of years during the war, assisiting in maintaining the bombes 24 hours a day.

The task was enlivened by the presence of the multitude of Wrens who operated the machines. No doubt they had volunteered for the Wrens in the expectation of the posting to a Royal Navy station with numerous handsome sailors. In reality, hundreds of them found themselves at Bletchley or its outstations working shifts over 24 hours a day, seven days a week, on arduous duties operating bombes.

They never complained, were always cheerful, conscientious and very patriotic, as well as being good fun off duty. The country's lasting gratitude goes to these young women, now elderly like myself, and to those no longer with us.'

After this diversion Jane Fawcett, MBE Hon FRIBA FSA, gives us a splendid overall decription of what working in 'the engine room' at Bletchley Park was actually like.

'Before joining Bletchley in February 1940 at the age of 19, I trained as a ballet dancer at Sadlers Wells under Ninette de Valois. This was an incredibly exciting period when the company was being formed; new ballets were appearing almost weekly and Frederick Ashton, Margot Fonteyn and Robert Helpman were emerging as great artists. We were taught by the famous Russian coach Sergeyev and by the great Ninette herself.

However, when the war began and many of my friends were called up, I decided to do a secretarial course in preparation for doing something useful. Soon after, two of my friends wrote from Bletchley to say they were seriously short of staff, that the work was important and encouraged me to join them. At about this time the German operational code, known as Enigma, had been cracked by the Bletchley codebreakers, and everything was taking off.

I was invited to go for an interview with Stuart Milner-Barry, a brilliant mathematician from Cambridge and the head of Hut 6. As there could be no advertising for staff, recruitment was done on a very personal level, and was even rather furtive and secretive. Milner-Barry was very shy and had no idea how to conduct an interview, but he did find out that I had learned some German (on a three month visit to Switzerland, just before the war), that I had done a secretarial course and that I had several friends already working at Bletchley. So he offered me a job - at a miserable salary - and took me to see the boss, Commander Denniston, who firmly explained that the work being carried out there was extremely important and highly secret, and that I had to sign the Official Secrets Act and never say anything about it - and I never have.

I was put into Hut 6, which was where the German Army operational code messages were decoded, processed, translated and distributed. I was very lucky to be there.

The hut consisted of the Preliminary Room in which incoming messages were received and processed. Next came the Registration Room, largely staffed by clever female graduates, known as the Blisters, many from Newnham College, Cambridge, where Milner-Barry's sister was Vice-Principal; then the Codebreakers Room where the most brilliant mathematicians worked. Had they not broken the Enigma code it is quite possible that we would not have won the war.

When they had broken the code for that day, they passed on the messages with the new settings to us in the Machine Room - working the Enigma machines. We had to decipher the coded messages and turn them into German. When I first arrived, there were only about nine of us acting as a link - unknown to the Germans - between German High Command and Whitehall. We worked three eight hour shifts, and often in times of crisis we worked sixteen hours, or even occasionally for twenty four hours at a time. Sleep seemed fairly irrelevant. Sometimes after a night shift I would catch the train up to London and meet Teddy' (later her husband). 'We used to go to HMV and shut ourselves in and listen to Mozart and fall in love - then return in the evening to work the night shift again.

When we had typed up and decoded the messages into German, some of which came directly from the German High Command, we handed them on to Hut 3 where the linguists lived; they had to translate them and determine the subject matter and decide which department in Whitehall to send them to. Some of the most urgent operational messages went directly to Churchill, to whom we had a direct line, both by telephone and teleprinter.'

Jane points out how Bletchley grew from 200 when she joined in 1940 to about 7000 when she left, many of them members of the WRNS, WAAF and ATS. 'Secrecy was instilled into all of us and the Germans never discovered what we were doing. It has been estimated that our work, and the fact that it was never revealed, shortened the war by two years or more and of course saved thousands of lives.

In September 1941 Churchill paid us a secret visit to thank us for our contribution to the war effort, and said 'You are the geese that laid the golden eggs and never cackled'. His visit gave us all a big boost and an incentive to work even harder.

Shortly before this, Milner-Barry and other senior staff members decided to write a letter to Churchill complaining about the under-staffing, poor accommodation and underequipment, all unacceptable considering the importance and urgency of our work. When Milner-Barry arrived at Number 10 and asked to see Churchill, he was asked who he was and what he wanted; unable to explain because of the Official Secrets Act, he had to leave the letter in his Private Secretary's hands, who promised to deliver it personally.

Churchill immediately issued one of his famous directives to General Ismay, Chief of General Staff, saying 'Make sure that they have all they want. Report to me that this has been done. Extreme priority'. Across it in his own hand he wrote 'Action this day'. Things improved from that moment on.

Up to this point I must tell you what conditions were like. We worked in large sheds, mostly without heating, though there were one or two coke boilers which smoked, so we had to open the windows to let out the smoke. The sheds had no insulation, concrete floors, windows covered in blackout material, trestle trables, collapsible chairs and unshaded light bulbs. They were hot in summer and very cold in winter when we worked in coats and mittens.

At night we had to fight our way in darkness, round the lake, through trees and bushes to the canteen in the big house, and through all this again to find our minibuses to take us home. My first billet was in a council house in Bletchley with a friendly young family. He was a driver for the London Brick Company under whose chimneys we lived; the acrid smell of brick smoke has remained with me ever since. The family had two small boys, both lively and noisy and not compatible with my need to sleep during the day. Eventually I was saved by some friends of my father, the Bonsor family, who lived in a magnificent neo-Elizabethan house, Liscombe Park near Leighton Buzzard. They invited me to bring one or two friends to live in their staff wing, which was then empty. This was a great improvement on the council house and we were very grateful, but we still had the noise problem as we were sleeping over the back door where all deliveries were made, wheelbarrows full of vegetables and the gardeners thumping their boots and banging the door. We also had a long walk in pitch black night to the pick up point for the minibus to take us to and from work; the whole countryside within a radius of 20 miles was serviced by a network of coaches and minibuses creeping along the lanes in the darkness. Some of the men were billeted in pubs and probably had more fun than we did. There was the Duncan Arms in Great Brickhill, which became known as the 'Drunken Arms', where some of our more spirited colleagues lived.

When we did have some leave I used my little motor bicycle, 'The Famous James', to get from Bletchley to Ugley in Essex where my family was living. This was a cross country journey through cornfields, and in the summer it was rather beautiful. However the two stroke engine was not designed for long journeys, and when the plugs heated up the engine stopped and I spent many hours sitting in a ditch while it cooled.

Because of the strict security we lived in a very tight community, a closed society where we made our own entertainments. We had a number of societies, which we founded and ran and to which most of us belonged. One of my favourites was the Scottish Dance Society run by an enthusiastic eccentric from Cambridge called Hugh Fosse. He dressed up for the part with a kilt and Scottish brogues, laced up over his calves. He was very tall and thin and pranced about demonstrating the dances with considerable spirit. As a dancer I thought he was wonderful. Then there was the Choral Society and the Drama Club, which put on plays and pantomimes - all good fun.

Rounders was also spirited but, as we had no posts, we had to use the trees round the front of the house as markers, which caused much merriment and arguments as to whether a player had reached the spruce or been caught out as he left the oak.

In spite of these diversions, our lives were much overshadowed by the knowledge that the faster we worked the more lives we might save, and the tension this produced affected us all, from the cryptographers and the girls in the machine room to the girls hammering out the messages and producing sense out of chaotic rubbish; from the translators turning cryptic messages into comprehensible language to those despatching them to the correct recipients; we were all on a knife edge, aware of the horrors threatening our very existence.

There had been a period when we had great difficulty in persuading the Admiralty that what we were telling them was really true, because it seemed so improbable that we should know in advance exactly what the Germans were going to do. When we told them that the *Scharnhorst* and the *Gneisenau* were coming out of the Baltic to attack our Fleet in the North sea, the Admiralty failed to believe us, and HMS *Glorious,* one of our vital aircraft carriers and two destroyers were sunk, with the loss of 1500 men. We felt very bitter about that.

The most thrilling night was the sinking of the *Bismarck*. She and the *Prinz Eugen* had come out to attack our shipping, sinking HMS *Hood* and badly damaging HMS *Prince of Wales*, and had then escaped and disappeared. I was on duty all that night and the next day, while we frantically tried to find out where she was going, so we could prevent her reaching safety in harbour. We picked up a message from the *Luftwaffe's* Chief of Staff, worried about his son who was serving in the *Bismarck*, asking where she was going. We intercepted the reply saying she was going to Brest. This time the Admiralty did believe us and she was attacked and sunk.

During the Blitz, we received the strategic orders from the *Luftwaffe* and were the first to intercept all their tactical orders on where and when to attack. This was one of our darkest hours when the Germans were carrying out systematic bombing attacks on many of our historic towns. We were crucially short of anti-aircraft guns, so if we were able to transmit the information about where the next attack was going to take place by lunchtime, it enabled Whitehall to order the transfer of the anti-aircraft equipment from say, Coventry, which had been attacked the previous night, to Plymouth which was planned for the following night. This might mitigate the force of the attack.

In July 1941 we at last managed to break the Naval Enigma code which carried information on all U-boat movements in the Atlantic. This saved one and a half million tons of shipping, thwarting the German's attempt to starve us to death, which at this time they were near to achieving.

In 1943 during the North African campaign we received advance warning of the movements of Rommel's supply convoys, on their way from Italy with reinforcements, allowing the RAF to sink many of them. We also informed Montgomery in advance about Rommel's movements in the field, enabling him to plan counter attacks. This was crucial to the defeat of the Africa Corps, which was a turning point in the war.

When it came to D-Day, Bletchley was much involved in deceiving the Germans about our invasion plans; as a result Rommel ordered two divisions to proceed from the Normandy beaches to the Pas de Calais region, enabling us to get our foothold during the vital first three days, while he struggled to return them to Normandy. A signal from Bletchley also diverted one of our airborne divisions from landing among the German troops.

After VE Day I was released and started my training to become a singer at the Royal Academy of Music. But, before leaving, I was interviewed by Commander Travis and asked to sign the Official Secrets Act again. His last words were: 'I cannot stress too highly the necessity for the maintenance of security; it is as vital as ever not to relax from the high standards of security that we have hitherto maintained. The temptation now to own up to our friends and families as to what our work has been is a very real one. It must be resisted absolutely.' And it was. End of story.'

Yet another young girl, who had worked at Bletchley on 'low-level' *Luftwaffe* codes and cyphers, felt that for some of the young people there, it was quite literally the time of their lives. 'I'm terribly grateful for the five years I had there. It was something quite out of this world. It was a very broadening experience, because of all these extraordinary people gathered together; many of us had come straight from school and were lifted up immediately into an atmosphere that perhaps we would never have met. Or that would only have come to us very, very slowly in our different lives. To be with people for whom books, music, art, history, everything like that was a daily part of their lives, it was an absolute blossoming for me, and I have to say that, though I have had many wonderful friends since, I've never again experienced that atmosphere of happiness, of enjoyment of everything that meant life to me.'

It is rather touching to read how so many young Wrens made their greatest permanent friends at that time, when they needed them most - after leaving home, often for the first time, and being plunged into communal life with complete strangers - finally sticking to each other all the sixty years since their Wren service. It is not easy, even now, to forget the mixed excitement and anguish of starting life in a new establishment. Would one be lucky enough to find a kindred spirit? We took our jobs extremely seriously and gladly endured considerable hardships, knowing that the men we were replacing were probably in much worse straits.

CHAPTER 20

—— ⚓ ——

MUTINY IN GIBRALTAR

An ex-Wren, and a friend of Sister Pamela Hussey, was not entirely sure whether to send her story, in case it was what she describes as 'Another Ra Ra, Jolly Hockey Sticks account of life in the war time WRNS, as if everything was superior, eminently harmonious and satisfactory. It wasn't.' Luckily she relented and sent her lively account:

Anne Glyn Jones, now a Research Fellow at Exeter University, had the most unusual experiences, perhaps the most fascinating occurred after her original training as a Wren Telegraphist when she was retrained to use Japanese morse for intercepting the Japanese Navy. She brilliantly recounts what happened to her in almost 'words of one syllable'. 'Japanese morse was, of course, completely different from European, since the Japanese do not use the Latin script. Their alphabet does not have separate symbols for consonants and vowels, but symbols that combine consonants and vowels. Thus (for instance) where the syllables TA, TE, TI, TO, TU would for us require combinations of six syllables, (AEIOU and T), the Japanese would need only five - but when one gets to the next group, MA, ME, MI, MO, MU, where Western morse needs only one more symbol, for M, the Japanese need five more, and so on through all the relevant letters of our alphabet.

Clearly it is impossible for a trained Western Telegraphist, so steeped in the code that no conscious intrusion was required to recognise what one was hearing (indeed if you couldn't momentarily recognise a symbol, you could watch your own hand write it, so complete was the ear-hand co-ordination, bypassing the conscious brain), it was impossible to unpick this training. So of course we had to interpret all morse symbols that we already knew with the letters we had always associated with them. A whole lot more written symbols had to be devised for all the extra morse symbols that we were now hearing. These we coped with mostly by the 'barred letter' symbol; for instance, we were accustomed to writing 'A' when we heard the symbol '*dit-dah*'. Now we were hearing '*dit-dah-dit-dah*'. This we would write as 'A' with a bar across the top, and so on with many other letters. With some of these new symbols we were already familiar, as the Germans used them in their call-signs, and to designate particular types of message (e.g. from a U-boat or a torpedo boat in coastal waters.) I think our 26-letter alphabet was transformed into a morse alphabet of over 60 characters in this way, but we had to supplement it with still more written symbols, e.g. a tent, or a tent on its side, or an 'L' written backwards.

Of course, the resulting written message was gibberish until someone had transcribed all our scribbles into the appropriate Japanese symbol, (the MA, or DO or RU, or whatever. MARU, incidentally, is Japanese for ship.) Even then the result was not Japanese language, as the original PL (plain language) would have been coded into meaningless sequences of syllables. This is where Bletchley took over. During the course of 1944 or early 1945, someone had the brilliant idea of producing typewriters in which the keyboard consisted of the symbols we were writing, but the actual striking keys typed the Japanese syllable. A whole stage of decoding eliminated at a stroke! Except that we, unlike American telegraphists, did not know how to type. We were given 24 hours of watchkeeping (i.e. a complete round of watches) in which to familiarise ourselves with the keyboards, (much bigger of course than the normal version) and then become operational. The Japanese, as I recall, were not prodigiously rapid transmitters, unlike some of the Germans, and especially the Italians, but even so finding and prodding the necessary key quickly enough was a colossal emotional strain. On a four-hour watch it was just about endurable, and fortunately for atmospheric reasons, during the long nine-hour night watches, the Far East usually faded out. I remember one flukey period in the early summer when the signals stayed in all night. After six or so hours I was trembling with nervous exhaustion, and called for a relief (a sailor with pencil took over from me) and I went outside and spent some minutes at dawn among the wild flowers outside our rural station. It was considered a pathetic confession of weakness, and I felt I had let the side down badly. When I felt sufficiently composed, I returned to the watch room, where I found my colleague on the other typewriter with her head on the keyboard weeping uncontrollably. I rather think this happened again the next night and after that they split the watch. The sailors took the view that we were feeble women - but none of the men ever got put on the typewriters. It wasn't the morse that defeated us....it was the typewriters.'

Anne also described her arduous year's service in Gibraltar and her exciting and unexpected journey back to England serving on board HMS *Ravager*. She continues: 'I am eternally glad that I was in the WRNS; to this day I count the friends I made in the WRNS among my closest and best. But I have never read a book about those days that wasn't smug, self-congratulatory and complacent. Everything hunky-dory, generating a certain resentment from the other women's services because they thought us so posh and pampered. Well, it wasn't like that at all - we had a very great deal to put up with. For the whole year in Gibraltar we were eaten by bed-bugs in our (duty) quarters on top of the Rock, fumigation being impossible because we shared our off-watch cabin with precious electrical equipment that kept the station functioning. Because no lights (including headlights) were allowed, except down in the town at sea-level (no point in blackout there when La Linea was blazing away next door, but the gun emplacements on the upper Rock were another matter). Transports could not operate on the dangerous roads of the upper Rock except in daylight hours, so the duty watches alternated by sleeping in turns in the cabin beside the watch-room. We had blankets and wooden pallets on the floor, where the infestation had established itself. We did our best with insecticide powders and requested iron bedsteads. Worse was to come. Huge rats (the hunt to kill them later became legendary) would invade our cabin and after one of us woke to find a rat chewing her hair, we virtually mutinied, and refused to return to work until we had beds (foolishly

152

thinking the rats would be deterred by the height of the bed). Our First Officer was surprised we had not got beds - she said she had ordered them when we first requested them. During my whole year on the Rock no officer ever came to inspect how we lived - if she had, she would have discovered we also entertained unwelcome rock apes in our quarters, who delighted in throwing our possessions down the rainwater catchments.

Our officers' neglect of our welfare was really galling - one of the weird things was that (all civilian women having been evacuated from the Rock) there was no source of sanitary towels. We had to get our families to post them out to us from England. Mercifully, at some stage Lord Nuffield took pity on us and provided us with a free issue.

We grew discontented and disgruntled, not least because, although we had been specially selected for overseas service, the girls at home had been rated Leading Rate, but we had not, though we had sat the exam before we left the UK. Attempts to remedy the situation were met by the assurance that there were no Y-Branch Telegraphists in Gibraltar, so the question of promotion did not arise. We sat the exams again but without recognition. Our discontents reached the Admiral himself. Fresh exams were prescribed (our third lot), much more difficult now, as they included elements of radio mechanics as well as telegraphy. Then the exigencies of the war changed and we were sent home (still unpromoted). We moved fairly rapidly to Portsmouth, Droxford, Chelmsford, London and Scarborough, training both as Petty Officers (though we were still not Leading Rates) and Japanese telegraphists. Weeks went by, and although we were assured that in the end we would get our back pay, (including 2d extra a day for proficiency in Japanese morse!) we were so poor we could not afford to go to the cinema, were still on the bottom rung and after three years we were still liable to scrub out the 'heads' (lavatories), and we did. There's much, much more to the extraordinary story of what the WRNS looked like when you were cynical and disillusioned, but it never interfered with our enthusiasm for our job or our pride in being associated with our beloved Royal Navy.'

Anne and her friends certainly did have a raw deal, but 'PS' she says, 'sometime in the spring of 1945 we got our hooks (!!) (Leading Wren badge), and actually ended our service as Petty Officers.'

Nevertheless it was a huge adventure which Anne describes, travelling home in HMS *Ravager*. 'The aircraft carrier was part of the escort of a convoy and when lurking U-boats in the middle of the Bay of Biscay caused 'action stations' to be called, all those Wrens who were available were sent to the sickbay prepared to nurse the wounded - as many of us, that is, as were not shut beneath the water-tight doors through being so exhausted after our year in Gib that they were asleep in their bunks. The exhaustion, incidentally, was not due to high jinks, but to the really debilitating tiredness caused by a year of averaging 5 hours sleep a night, and our Nissen huts, which leaked in the winter and roasted in the summer, being shared with day workers who could not remember that watch-keepers needed to sleep during the day. The MO started hurried First Aid instruction, but I think it was just as well there were no wounded to depend on our ignorance, however well-intentioned, of things medical.'

Anne comments finally that 'For anyone who thinks that the modern girls were the first to serve at sea, it is a fact that we, in our skirts (one did not appear in public in bell-bottoms), were manning the decks of the carrier, along with the sailors as we came into port up the Clyde. *Ravager*, incidentally, was a rather unsteady ship, though whether she was a banana boat, (laid down as something else, with a flight deck added during construction), or a *Woolworth* carrier (always destined to be a carrier, but on the cheapest, quickest possible production lines), I now forget. Everything on board clanged, it seemed to be made entirely of metal; anyway it didn't seem to take all that much of a sea for her to plunge like a bucking bronco, and the sick-bay where we sat awaiting the wounded was right up in the plunging bows.'

It is a sad loss that no-one can produce a picture of what must have been a most memorable sight - Wrens in their skirts, manning the side, as the *Ravager* sailed up the Clyde.

CHAPTER 21

——— ⚓ ———

BOATING WRENS

One of the most sought after jobs you could have in the WRNS was to be a Boating Wren. These much envied girls sported the most defining emblem - the white lanyard - and were allowed to wear bell-bottoms (which made everyone else very jealous.) They worked 24 hour watches and transformed the harbours of Plymouth and Portsmouth into the most welcoming and attractive ports for our war weary sailors.

We probably know Diana Luck quite well now through her letters in this book, so here is the promised masterpiece, 'Twenty four hours in the Life of a Plymouth Boating Wren' - sounding as fresh as the day she penned it all those years ago.

'Someone's alarm screams into the early morning, and the six occupants of no 8 cabin begin their day. The crews of our boat *Black Bat* change watches at 0900, so I can safely snatch another hour in bed.

It is necessary to plan carefully what to take for a 24 hour shift when one is supposed to maintain a fairly smart appearance. As I stuff things into my already bulging bag, I mutter 'clothes brush, hair-brush, shoe brush, toothbrush, book, pencil, cigarettes, powder, lipstick, soap, sponge, towel'....a glance out of the window shows a tattered grey sky....westerly wind, probably rain....oilskin, sou'wester. With all my gear laid ready on the bed (bottom half of a double decker) I run up to the end house of the row of eight which forms the WRNS Quarters. This is the mess, and here a vast number of people are rapidly consuming cornflakes and condensed milk, limp-looking sausages and mugs of tea. Barbara, our Leading Wren Coxswain, joins me and together we start on our one and half mile walk to the dockyard. There are little slummy shops all the way down Stoke Hill, and our bags become heavier as we keep popping into, first, a chemist for Rose Hip Syrup or cough drops, then a greengrocer for carrots or tomatoes, then a dairy for milk - very Black Market. As we draw nearer the dockyard, we meet tired grimy boaters coming off duty, wearily trudging up the hill. We stop at the paper man at the dockyard gate. 'Got a *Times* for you dearie,' he says, thrusting a copy at me, 'the Commodore's gone on leave'. We plod on, past wet and dry docks, past destroyers, minesweepers, corvettes and occasionally a battleship or aircraft carrier in for a refit. Skilfully we dodge lorries, staff cars, motor bicycles and trains, which career up and down with no respect for the rule of the road. Eventually to a fanfare of loud catcalls and whistles, we arrive at HMS *Derwent*. The moment we are sighted, our opposite numbers (who have to wait on board until we arrive on duty,) scuttle up the gangway and disappear.

Our boat is a 38 ft open Naval Cutter with a petrol Kelvin Engine. She is the runabout for the Officers of the Coastal Forces - MTBs, MLs, and RMLs which are either based on or visiting HMS *Derwent*. We run regular trips at set times from the Base to HMS *Defiance*, which is the control for operations, repairs, pay etc, and is also a training ship for some 1500 electrical and torpedo specialists; she is anchored about a mile upstream, and the trip takes us about 15 minutes.

Soon Irene, the stoker, turns up with Maria, the blue-eyed deck-hand, who ought not to be allowed to wear bell-bottoms. Irene, a dazzling blonde, who in peacetime sewed corsets in Wigmore Street, has a hangover. She disappears under the awning which covers the engine, and amidst a flow of profanity, kicks the engine into activity. Barbara, who received orders from the Officer of the Watch, and a reprimand for forgetting to call him 'Sir,' leaps on board and yells 'Leggo forrard, leggo aft' to Maria and me, and 'Slow astern stokes' to Irene. We are carrying one small frightened looking Sub Lieut and a bundle of mail. I am sternsheetsman. Maria is crouched up in the bows clutching a boathook, Irene is gloomily sitting on her little stool in front of the engine, and Barbara is steering from the stern; of course, standing on a box to increase her height. Frequently she hands the tiller to me when she wants to read her book, or go to sleep on long trips. I shall be a coxswain myself in three weeks' time. One has to steer our boat with the tiller between one's knees, or with a foot, and in heavy weather or when turning in a strong current we can only get her round by combined efforts.

We pass the balloon barrage and exchange frantic waves and back-chat with the skipper, who is an old friend. As we chug smoothly upstream we look around for new arrivals and departures of familiar ships. 'Revenge has gone' Irene mourns, thinking of the loss of a jitter-bugging leading seaman. 'Couple of new Yank sloops', squeaks Maria from the bows. We gaze in admiration at the long, lean grey-hound shapes moored side by side; the entire crews, including officers, seem to be lined up against the rail to watch us pass. 'They must be new' we remark scornfully. *Defiance* is in sight, and we all screw up our eyes to read the large lettered notice on her stern. It is common knowledge to all who work in ships that one brings a craft alongside its destination against the flow of the tide. 'Ebb!' we shout simultaneously. This free information is a new gesture on the part of their Lordships. We used to have to work it our for ourselves, always too late of course, and usually leading to an amateurish change of course in mid-stream. HMS *Defiance*, which is three old battleships, is moored about 100 yds from the Cornish shore of the river.

The traffic in this narrow strip of water becomes very congested and the negotiations of bringing the boats alongside the main gang-way is a nightmare to any coxswain. Barbara pales somewhat, and presses the button for the hooter as an enormous NAAFI tug bears down upon us. A black hairy face is poked out of the wheelhouse as they thunder past. 'Learn the rule of the road!' yells an angry voice. 'They don't seem to like women' says Irene, who has been doing her stuff from amidships. The sight of her yellow head usually calms the most irate sea captain.

'Captain's barge!', someone screams. Barbara utters a word that would have made her mother wince, and gives the order to 'GO SLOW!' and stand to attention. This is not easy, as we are rolling about in the gigantic wash of the NAAFI boat. The Captain's barge, shining with cleanliness, her brass funnel winking in the sun, glides by. I catch a glimpse of the Captain, small and lonely in the stern, drooping over his morning paper.

We tie up alongside the gangway, and the Sub, (our passenger, whom we had forgotten) crawls out stammering thanks. 'You're welcome, chum,' says Barbara, taking grave risks, for subs can have a sting in their tail. We return to Base without passengers, Full Speed Ahead, and lustily singing our large repertoire of bawdy songs. Now we have half an hour to wait, so in pairs we take it in turns to go to the Submarine Base canteen, where apart from the usual canteen merchandise we can occasionally buy dates and peanuts. One of the ML crews has brewed tea, and they send us down a jug.

On the next trip we take 4 officers; one of them is a friend of ours and comes into the stern with us and tells us libellous Coastal Forces gossip as we are on our way. By now it is nearly noon so we think of lunch. On reaching the Main Gangway we tie up as is customary, with half an hour to wait. '*Black Bat II!*', yells a voice from the top of the gangway steps. The Master at Arms is standing there with a megaphone at his lips. 'Moor aft and tie up along Gash Shoot.' We groan. The Gash Shoot is a hole in the side of the ship through which they tip all the rubbish and garbage. There is a narrow and dangerous ladder by the side of it, and a floating catamaran at the bottom to which we have to tie the boat. We hate it. The catamaran sinks a bit when one steps on it and foul refuse-filled water slops over one's feet. The ladder is extremely dizzy-making and very slippery. The whole place smells of decaying filth, and so often we are ordered there to make room for bigger and more important boats. A crowd of torpedo ratings off duty watch our ascent, with cheers and boos almost reducing us to tears of rage.

In order to reach the Wren's quarters we have to descend countless iron steps, rattle down endless dark, narrow corridors, crawl through numerous low doorways, fall over inexplicable rings, knobs, hooks, posts, and bump our heads on every conceivable contraption that protrudes from above. We proceed in single file, at the double, colliding with the odd 200 ratings coming the other way.

WRNS Quarters consists of three cabins; one where we sit, one where the day workers sit and eat their sandwiches (this is where we sling our hammocks at night) and one mess. In addition to this a re three tiny cabins for the Duty Wrens, one bathroom and one lavatory.

Between 1200 and 1300 hours some 45 Wrens congregate to wash, powder their noses, eat, smoke, chatter and play the wireless. We boaters invariably arrive at the tail end of lunch and have to fight our way in to the mess to seize a plateful of unappetising left-overs. We hardly have time to swallow this before the loud-hailer blares out over the general noise 'Away - *Black Bat II!*'. We grab our hats, seize a hunk of bread and run. Irene wails that she must spend a penny. Maria has lost her gloves, but we cannot stop. A fierce-looking officer waits impatiently on the main gangway while we move forward from the Gash Shoot.

The afternoon is more peaceful. We have a 40 minute wait at the Base during which we brew coffee on a Primus stove. Then our peace is shattered by the embarking of the Coastal Forces football team. We have to take them down the Hameoaze to a football ground near Trevoll. This a long trip, and highly popular as we carry no officers. Off come our hats, anyone can take the helm, we wave and shout at tugs and battleships alike as we career at high speed on our drunken-looking course.

Having dropped the team, we then make for Cremyll Pier to the petrol barge from which we refuel. A genial civilian called Andy serves us, chatting the while in broad Cornish. He laboriously writes out a chit in triplicate and hands one to Irene. I asked her once what she did with them. 'Wait till I've got a round dozen, then chuck 'em overboard', she replied. On our return trip to Trevoll, we pass an American harbour craft who hails us with an invitation to icecream and coffee - we accept; the Americans, although they are only tugmen, live in a wonderful way. They are highly intrigued with us 'sailor girls', and we have difficulty in getting away. As we go, they shower us with gifts of chewing gum, Lucky Strike, oranges and an enormous tin of Fruit Cocktail which we know from experience is delicious.

The football team are hot and dirty, and their muddy boots create havoc on our decks. It starts to rain and the wind against the tide sets up a short choppy sea. No-one volunteers to take the tiller now, and Barbara goes on strike so I take over. A gloom has descended on passengers and crew alike, they all huddle in the bottom of the boat trying to keep dry from the rain and the spray of the breaking waves. When the team have disembarked at the Base we take four magnificent bearded Lieutenants to *Defiance* and tie up to the Main Gangway, casting a baleful eye at the Master at Arms who actually lets us stay. We have about four minutes in which to drink a cup of cold tea. This next trip is the last routine one, and we thankfully anticipate our evening. Barbara says she will wash her hair. This is the day workers leave at 5.30, so we practically have the place to ourselves in the evenings if we are there. I shall go up to the School room on the Upper Deck, open to all, where I can play gramophone records of any symphony or concerto. Irene and Maria have arranged to go to the ship's dance with two killicks from the Torpedo School. The trip to Base is unpleasant, we are wet, cold and tired. It is still raining and the sea is still choppy. Irene moans about the leaking awning which is sure to cause a breakdown in the engine. The Officer of the Watch calls Barbara for orders. We wait in trepidation, anxious eyes turned towards his cabin. She stumps back with a face of thunder, holding her thumbs down. 'Got to return here as soon as we have had supper and take six of them up the Tamar to Cargreen pub. Hell!' We are sad, but there it is, 24 hours on duty is 24 hours on duty. Supper will be cold spam and bored-looking beetroot - it always is on dance nights, and there won't be time to change or dry our clothes.

Back on *Defiance* I am cheered by dear Cookie, who grabs me with an enormous hairy hand as we pass the Wardroom Galley. 'Got some prunes for 'ee', he croaks, handing me a vast pudding bowl of fat juicy prunes obviously destined for the wardroom table; all one ever sees of Cookie, bless him, is two beady black eyes looking through a hatch and an out-thrust fist, rarely without some titbit. Irene and I consume the prunes, spitting the stones out through the porthole. Barbara eats no supper, and is soon lying back in her chair with a paper-white face. She is subject to these knockout attacks, either as a result of unsuitable food or overstrain, and unless we insist on her stopping she will struggle on more dead than alive. We sling her hammock for her, roll her in blankets and push her in.

I am now responsible for the boat, crew and passengers. The Officer of the Watch at the Base scrutinises me, one characteristic eyebrow shooting up into his scalp. 'You all right to take over?' I hastily assure him, and we set off with six very young, very jolly Sub Lieutenants; this long trip up the River Tamar can be very lovely on a fine evening. From Brunel's Bridge at Saltash onwards there is unspoilt Devon countryside on either side of the bank, but tonight, with poor visibility, a nasty cross wind and choppy water it is anything other than pleasant.

The boat somehow seems inadequately manned, with only three of us. Maria looks very small and young. I peer through a hole in the awning at Irene and see a reassuring unconcerned bulk engrossed in a tome called *Blood on her Shoe*; she looks round and catches my eye. 'What'll you do when it's dark?' she queries, knowing I have never coxswained a boat after sundown. 'The Devil looks after his own,' I reply with a confidence unfelt. It is pitch dark when we start for home, and the boys are exceedingly merry. Maria, after fixing the riding light, comes to stand very close to me and we creep forward into the baffling darkness. Soon, we see lights both moving and stationary, coloured and non-coloured, and Maria and I have conflicting ideas as to their meaning, some seem uncomfortably near. 'That is either a vessel not under command, or a vessel employed in laying telegraph cables, under way' I assert, taking a wide sweep inshore at the risk of running into the mud. Irene's head appears. 'Isn't that a Steam Patrol Vessel at anchor? Oh, for a Seamanship Manual.' Gingerly we chug on; our passengers are singing a Coastal Forces version of *The Farmer's Boy*, fortissimo, effectively drowning all the warning hooters and shouts I fully expect to hear. The river seems interminable, and although Maria's teeth are chattering, I feel extraordinarily warm.

We become accustomed to the darkness and bravely increase speed. Huge fantastic shapes loom up and disappear, and all lights are given a wide berth, with Maria feebly poking the water with a boathook in case we hit the bank. Somehow, hours later, we bump gently against the friendly side of the *Derwent*. Totally unaware of the dangers through which they have come, our passengers bid us farewell. 'Carry on Coxswain' an inebriated voice calls. As if in a dream or nightmare, I head vaguely in the direction of *Defiance*. We can hear something big and powerful throbbing upstream. There are two moving lights across our bows. 'That might be two ships or both ends of one ship,' we say (or forty six other things). I don't know. But I have beginner's luck, for soon there is an unmistakable darker darkness and a light over the water showing up *Defiance's* stern anchor cable.

We've made it. The relief makes me unwontedly cheeky to the Quartermaster on the Gangway, who is bored, but he still fetches up cups of 'kye', that delicious sickly beverage beloved of all sailors.

We sling our hammocks, and it seems about ten minutes before I hear the raucous voice over the loudhailer about eight inches from my ear. 'All the hands, all the hands, lash up and stow, lash up and stow. Captains of Heads fill gravity tanks'. We have never discovered the exact meaning of this last statement, but know it has something to do with the lavatories. This is followed by a piercing blast on the bosun's pipe, and the mad scramble begins. We have to be at the Base by 0650 for the first trip. Irene is always last, and morning after morning we stand panting on the boat, unsuccessfully attempting to start the engine, while she strolls down the gangway tugging a comb through her hair with a persuasive flick, and as the usual burst of blasphemy starts up, away we go.

In spite of the rush and the cold and the empty stomach, I love this early trip, and there is something impressive and breathtaking about the dark trails of smoke from factory chimneys and ships' funnels across the clear dawn sky; the anchored vessels have a luminous unreal quality. Even in mid-river, the air smells of damp earth and gardens and wood smoke, and I have a sudden longing to be on land. We take a load of sleepy cross maintenance men from the Base Pier to various MTBs, then dash back to *Defiance* for breakfast. I can rarely face the mad scramble, and rely on some kind soul to bring me a mug of tea and a marmalade sandwich. Then we slip across the narrow stretch of water to Wilcove Pier right opposite *Defiance*, where we pick up our CO who lives on the Cornwall side. He is very grand and remote, and after acknowledging the Coxswain's salute takes no further notice of us. But he always brings his Golden Cocker Spaniel with him, to whom we are deeply attached. Our friends en route, the ballroom man and others, wave wildly at us shouting bawdy greetings, and look a little downcast when we fail to reply - until they see, led by pointed gestures from Barbara, the gold lace on the cap of our passenger.

And so the circle is complete. After half an hour, surely the longest in the twenty four, we see the wonderful figures of their other watch tripping down the *Derwent*'s ladder - then we too become tired and dirty 'boaters', trudging wearily up Stoke Hill.'

CHAPTER 22

THE SPRINGBOARD OF ATTACK

In between all the official and warlike Combined Operations was a more personal, celebratory and peaceful combined operation, when John and I were married in London. Working on the estimated possible date of *Oribi's* next boiler clean, 15th December 1943, my mother had taken a huge gamble in complete confidence, regardless of the Admiralty, the war and any other extraneous circumstances. She had booked the church, St James, Spanish Place, the reception at the English Speaking Union, ordered the cake to be made by Searcys

Christian and John on their wedding day

(of Sloane St) with black market dried fruit, extracted clothes coupons from anyone she could browbeat into parting with them, bought me a trousseau of garments she hoped would fit and I would like, and finally acquired a secondhand, white velvet wedding dress; this she acquired from an advertisement in the *Country Gentleman's Association Magazine* for £6 I think (no coupons required for second hand objects), it was also not tried on as I was still in Belfast. She had then sent out the invitations and sat back with her fingers crossed, and hey presto, by the greatest good luck the bridegroom appeared. We were lent a small green Austin 7 for our honeymoon; and our send off, driving it away in style, was spectacular.

163

Immediately after this, *Oribi* was sent to Falmouth for further repairs. My kind friend, Chief Officer Nancy Osborne at Headquarters (whom I had so fortuitously met in the coal hole when I was under threat from Miss Buckmaster) and who still had my welfare at heart, appointed me as temporary supernumerary to the plot at Falmouth. Here I was rather welcomed, as it meant we worked in five watches instead of four and had a little more breathing space. John had arrived first and cleverly found us a kindly farmer's wife who lent us half her house. 'I got a Jersey cow to make some Cornish cream for 'ee', she said, appreciating the lack of such luxury in our diet. It was an idyllic week or two post honeymoon, though perhaps a little lacking in mod cons. The privy was at the bottom of the garden, and with its half door gave you a wonderful view of luscious green fields of burgeoning spring, and if you were very lucky, a visit from the doe-eyed Jersey cow who would come to view these strange foreigners who had invaded the back garden which was her home. Baths were available in a tin tub in front of the kitchen fire, which was a new and rather jolly experience for us both.

The plot at Falmouth, which came under the Commander in Chief Western Approaches, and which I already knew, was very exciting. So much activity was taking place as the war hotted up. A great many German E-boats would dash over and do as much damage as possible to any shipping, either in the Channel, or, very cheekily, nearer our coasts and ports. These were usually picked up by the radar plot, and action would be ordered to pursue them. By this time we had invented the Magnetron radar and this gave us an extraordinary high degree of plotting precision.

Without going into the mammothly complicated Admiralty organisation of the Navy, I found it fascinating to discover (again from Patrick Beesly's book *Very Special Intelligence*) that plots were becoming essential in most operational departments, and the need to have a Master Plot for all our own vessels, with executive powers and working closely with Operational Intelligence Centre (part of DNI, Director of Naval Intelligence, Rear Admiral John Godfrey) whose own plot showed estimates of the enemy's dispositions, became obvious. The Operations and Trade plots were amalgamated (under the command of Commander RA Hall RN) and housed in a large room next door to the Tracking Room (Rodger Winn). All routes, both for warships and merchantmen, were now prepared by the Main Plot Staff, and all diversions of convoys and independent ships in the Atlantic were initiated by them, working in co-operation with C-in-C Western Approaches, who controlled the escort forces. Hall and Winn were both masterful personalities, but worked in the closest possible partnership. Admiral Edelsten (Assistant Chief of Staff U-boats and Trade) gave orders in 1943 that no ships were ever to be routed against the advice of the Tracking Room, without his own express permission. When things went wrong there was no backbiting; all Hall's energies would be concentrated on trying to extricate his precious ships from whatever new danger had beset them. Rodger Winn was a remarkable man. He had been thwarted in his first ambition to join the Royal Navy by an acute attack of polio which left him with a twisted back, but he had become a successful barrister, and in 1939, at the age of thirty seven, he volunteered as an interrogator of prisoners of war, but was luckily diverted to Naval Intelligence. Here he became almost legendary with his brilliant ability to see into the mind of the German High Command, and his total dedication to the Tracking Room, working all hours of the day and night. Such was his merit that Admiral Godfrey arranged for him to be commissioned in the RNVR. To commission a civilian to head such a vital department was unprecedented, and eventually he was promoted Captain RNVR, OBE, CB and awarded the American Legion of Merit, returning to the Bar after the war. Admiral Edelsten writes of him, 'His experience, wisdom and sound appreciation of the U-boat war have saved this country a vast amount of shipping tonnage, and enabled a heavy toll to be taken of U-boats on many occasions. It is not an exaggeration to say that his work is of national importance and very ably shouldered.'

Rear Admiral John Godfrey, as Director of Naval Intelligence, was responsible for the rebuilding of this important division, personally handpicking his staff. He was, according to Patrick Beesly in *Very Special Admiral*, 'a practical and successful seaman, a somewhat unusual naval officer of wide interests, great energy and determination, an innovator and original thinker and not one of those who considered that what was good enough for Nelson was necessarily good enough for the Royal Navy of 1939.' From the same source we learn that Godfrey had several brushes with Winston Churchill, which may well have been one of the reasons for the astounding, not to say shameful, lack of any recognition of his immense services during the war, an omission which was, incidentally, deeply resented by every member of the Intelligence Division.

Plotting Wrens had first been employed in 1941, but soon there were Plotting Officers, and every operations room had its own plot. It became more and more essential for planning an operation or for viewing an up to date picture of an ongoing battle; important plots were kept up to five minutes accuracy, and the value of this was plain to see as more and more senior staff would pay frequent visits. Plymouth was my first experience of Combined Operations, and later I was to be appointed to the Headquarters in Whitehall, preparing very secret documents for the landings of D-Day.

After the remarkable recovery from the debacle of Dunkirk, we were lucky to have our Prime Minister, Mr Winston Churchill, to rally our shocked spirits and prepare us for eventual victory. It never once occurred to me - or anyone I knew, that we could possibly lose the war, but it was very cheering to listen to his speeches about blood, sweat and tears, which were clearly going to be needed if we were to follow Churchill, who had ordered the south coast of England to turn 'from a bastion of defence to a springboard of attack'.

The Combined Operations Command was formed in 1940 with the three services, to provide training in amphibious warfare, which comprised all kinds of offensive action from small raids to large assault landings on enemy coasts. Its job was to produce the plans, the special types of craft required, and above all, the closest spirit of co-operation, creating in its Combined Training Centres a mix of sailor-soldiers, soldier-sailors, and airmen soldiers who had a complete understanding of each other's methods and problems.

The research into future operations began immediately after the fall of France, when our enemies held all the coasts of Western Europe (save those of Portugal and Spain) who were established in North Africa and Abyssinia and were soon to master Yugoslavia, Crete and Greece; it must have seemed to Hitler that nothing could stop him taking Britain next, and then Russia. It was the brilliant victory by the Royal Air Force of the Battle of Britain that forced him to change his mind and invade Russia first, thereby giving us the time (at what was perhaps the most crucial moment of our history) to consider ways of counter attack. About a week after Dunkirk, the Commandos were formed to carry out such irregular warfare; guerrilla tactics were just what was demanded for this situation, for our frame of mind and for an idea which strongly commended itself to our Prime Minister. Commandos were all soldiers who had already passed through the rigorous training by our army, but upon whom a special emphasis of individual initiative was superimposed. As an example, a troop might have come off parade at 3pm and was then told to be on duty at 6am the following morning at a place perhaps a hundred miles away. How that Commando got there was up to him, but get there at the appointed time he must. His officers did just as he did, but always a little better, establishing respect and confidence in his leaders, and he was encouraged to put forward at once any good practical suggestions as how to improve his own performance, which would be considered for the common good Operations started with a few raids by a few men on unimportant enemy posts - and the first of these took place on 23rd June, only 19 days after Dunkirk - building up until the great raid of St Nazaire and later Dieppe.

The gallant and enterprising attack on St Nazaire would succeed in inflicting very serious damage on our enemy's Naval facilities. It was the most exciting action for us Wren plotters to follow and it was rather like living through a particularly sensational action film, but it was real and it was happening now. Plotting Officers saw the signals as the plan unfolded and our plot covered the whole arena.

Only the French west coastal ports of Brest and Lorient could rival the importance of St Nazaire as a Naval base for forces engaged in the Battle of the Atlantic, so it was a most important target. Once the Bismarck was gone, there were only three enemy-held ports in the whole world where her sister ship, the *Tirpitz*, could dock: Singapore, Genoa, and the most serious for us, St Nazaire, with its huge dry dock, the Forme Ecluse, which was over 1,100 feet long. *Tirpitz* was now the biggest threat to our shipping and in spite of three costly bombing raids, in port we had failed to sink her; how could we spike her guns? We could remove the only refuge for *Tirpitz*, should she

require repairs away from her German North Sea base. St Nazaire
has other docks and locks through which ships up to 10,000 tons
could enter, and directly opposite the old entrance were the massive
submarine pens, with nine completed and five under construction at
this point and the great Forme Ecluse lying at the SE corner at an
angle of about 45 degrees. Sandwiched between the waters of the
harbour and the river Loire, with its power stations, pumping
machinery and other lock installations and warehouses, the Old
Town of St Nazaire itself covered no more than one square mile and
was an area as closely defended as any along the whole western
seaboard of German occupied Europe. It was against these formidable
ramparts that one of the most hazardous and successful experiments
in the history of Combined Operations was launched.

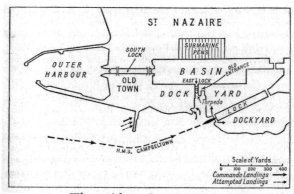

The raid on St. Nazaire

From the beginning, the destruction of the Forme Ecluse by
ramming it with one of our destroyers was the main objective,
followed by the disablement of as much as possible of the other locks
and installations, and eventually further wreckage in the U-boat area.
There was one serious objection from the Commander in Chief,
Plymouth, who was convinced that the ship would bounce off the
lock gate instead of jamming in it. Even when confronted with the
engineer who had constructed the lock gate and who sided with the
planners, he refused to budge from his opinion. Mountbatten dug his
toes in, and the raid went ahead. HMS *Campbeltown*, a former
American destroyer, commanded by Lt Commander SH Beattie, was

chosen as the weapon of destruction, to be escorted by two Hunt Class destroyers, HMS *Atherstone* and HMS *Tynedale*, a Motor Gun Boat, a Motor Torpedo Boat and a number of Motor Launches - four of which carried torpedoes - and the remainder of the military force (mostly transported by the destroyers). This consisted of 44 officers and 224 soldiers of Number 2 Commando. The Naval Force was to be commanded by Commander RED Ryder RN, awarded the VC for this action, in peacetime an Antarctic explorer and winner of the Polar Medal. The Military Force leader was Lt Colonel AC Newman, the Essex Regiment (also awarded the VC), commanding No 2 Commando. Surprise was vital, and a diversionary air raid tactic was arranged to disguise the noise of ships' engines and distract the defenders' guns. Each demolition party with its protection party had exact instructions: with the successful completion of demolition work, in particular the blowing up of the bridges, this would convert the dock area into an island so as to thwart any enemy concentration and withdrawal would follow. Two hours was the maximum time allowed for the Military Force to complete its operation, by which time the Naval Force would have to leave in order to get clear before daybreak and regain the escorting destroyers.

An elaborate system of time fuses was arranged in the *Campbeltown* which made possible the blowing up of five tons of explosive, after allowing first for her impact with the lock and then for her scuttling. This task was entrusted to Lieut HT Tibbetts RN, who was awarded the DSC for a feat which was described by Commander Ryder 'as both original and brilliant', and as covering the Force Commanders 'against a whole multitude of circumstances we could not foresee.'

The Naval Force left Falmouth harbour in late afternoon of March 1942. The operation room plot was alive with anticipation (I was still at C in C Plymouth at that time). There was no advance warning of any specific danger ahead, and the cruising order of the expedition was in three columns, the port and starboard consisting of the motor launches, and the midships of the two Hunt class destroyers with *Campbeltown* astern. The weather was fine, and air cover was provided until out of range. The detecting of a submarine was a first threat, but upon Tynedale opening fire she crash dived, and after a pattern of depth charges she was heard of no more; two French trawlers were sighted, but Commander Ryder reports 'they legged it at such a rate I felt confident they had not sighted our force'. Two further trawlers were sighted, and after removing their crews, papers and charts they we re sunk by gunfire. 'C'est la guerre' said the skipper of one, philosophically. By 11pm, after having been at sea for 33 hours, the force was brought by the most brilliant and daring navigation on the part of Lieut AR Green RN, Force Navigation Officer, to exactly the right place at exactly the right time. The planned air raid took place and 'the sky was lit with a veritable firework display of blue green and white tracer from the German AA guns.' Inevitably, the enemy was soon aroused, and eve ry available searchlight concentrat e d on the estuary, floodlighting the entire force - 'each boat' writes Captain Ryder in a riveting contemporary account, 'with her silvery white bow and stern wave clearly visible, and with the *Campbeltown* astern of us rising up above all the others.'

This picture (and the one on page 172) were drawn by Commander Ryder VC in command of the Naval Force. Above is the MGB, with the Force Commanders on board, under fire from a flak position on top of a petrol storage depot. Behind the Campbeltown can be seen the pump house, later blown up by the landing parties; and in the distance, beyond her stern, is the outline of the concrete submarine pens. On the left, MLs carrying Commando troops are fighting their way towards the Old Entrance.

·The glare of a disturbed enemy was upon us. A few moments later a dozen searchlights caught her, the period of stealth was at an end and all was now sound and fury.'

From the frenzy of the next two hours the atmosphere is best recaptured from the accounts of those who came back, mostly pieced together in their own words. Lieut Curtis describes how the MGB rushed past him at 18 knots. 'I could then see that *Campbeltown* was being hit very frequently, especially on the bridge.

Her engine room appeared to be on fire, stuff was going off in every direction and the noise was very great. We saw the entrance to the lock, put our helm down to starboard to let the *Campbeltown* go ahead; she was coming fast and shooting hard; she made a straight dive for the lock gates and she had to help her a flood tide of towards one and a half knots. There was the hell of a crash.'

Commander Ryder, who was standing next to Lieut Curtis, describes how 'she was lost to us in the glow of searchlights as we circled round to starboard. The next we saw of her was at the moment of her striking the lock gates. There was a grinding crash and the flash of some minor explosion on her foc's'le as she came to rest.We were unable to see the soldiers scrambling ashore but we could see she remained fast in the gate with all her guns firing hard up the lock.' The plan laid down that the *Campbeltown* should hit the lock gate at 1.30am. She hit it at 1.34am. She rammed and stuck good and hard in the lock gates – their designer had been right.

'The cool precision and daring with which Lieut Commander Beattie (also awarded the VC) and his men carried out this formidable order has rarely been surpassed in the annals of the Navy. Never has a British destroyer been 4 minutes late for a rendezvous with such glorious and devastating effect.' So says the contemporary official account written by the Ministry of Information. If only they had been able to transmit it live on CNN - if only there could have been satellite communication - if only. Even so, there could have been few more thrilling and thrilled vicarious spectators that day than ourselves, huddled round our operational plot.

Through all this mayhem, the men in the engine room of the Campbeltown, in all the heat and darkness, stoked the furnaces to the maximum, right up to the moment of impact. Orders were then given to abandon ship, and the Chief Engineer, Artificer H Howard, now had to take charge of the difficult scuttling operation. With all the lights in the ship gone and steam shut off, the task had to be carried out by torchlight. 'No time could be wasted and I had to get busy opening valves etc to flood the ship'. The ship was partly on fire, but making his way through the flames on the upper deck and collecting several of his shipmates, they scrambled down the ladders placed by the Commandos and got ashore. A series of loud explosions from the area of the Forme Ecluse proved that the Commandos were carrying out their orders of demolition.

The MGB, with Commander Ryder and Lieuts Curtis and Green, was the last boat to leave the scene. They made a final effort to contact the forces ashore, but there was a fierce battle in progress, and because it was impossible to distinguish friend from foe in the dark turmoil they could not join safely.

The escape of the MGB was almost a miracle. She is depicted (above) as severely damaged, she ran down the Loire at 24 knots with searchlight beams full upon her, under heavy fire from both banks.

Their escape was almost a miracle; the MGB sped down the river at 24 knots with searchlight beams full on them and accurate fierce fire from both banks. For 25 minutes they faced the onslaught with the indefatigable Gunner Savage at the pompom maintaining continuous fire. Commander Ryder recalls the tragedy: 'it was the last salvo of all which straddled us in the dark at a range of about four miles and to our great sorrow a splinter struck and killed Able Seaman Savage.' He was awarded the VC 'for his great gallantry, skill and devotion to duty'. Besides the VCs to Commander Ryder and Lt Commander Beattie (who was taken prisoner) 14 DSCs were also awarded. The casualties were high. 34 officers were killed out of 62, of ratings 151 out of 291; but when the *Campbeltown* finally detonated her delayed explosives, she took with her an inspection party of some 40 senior German officers and about 400 soldiers and sightseers who were swarming round the dock area. It is estimated that another 400 or so Germans were mown down by each other in the general mêlée, the German khaki being mistaken for British battledress. 'Manoeuvre Well Executed', as they say in the Navy; the *Tirpitz* guns were seriously spiked.

CHAPTER 23

$$\text{⚓}$$

BACK TO FRANCE AT LAST

Ever since Mountbatten's personal summons from the Prime Minister to take over the Command of Combined Operations in October 1941, the total focus was to be the re-invasion of France. His orders were to forget about the defensive; his whole attention was to be concentrated on the offensive.

Mountbatten was a brilliant man, and his career in the Royal Navy had been meteoric and very much based on his passion for communications. He had specialised in signals, taking the Higher Wireless course at Greenwich and coming top; he was then appointed Senior Instructor and wrote the first comprehensive textbook on all the wireless sets in the Navy. With this high level of technical knowledge and grasp of detail, he was appointed Fleet Wireless Officer, and was thus responsible for the communications throughout the entire Fleet. His mastery of this

Admiral Lord Louis Mountbatten

important organisation enabled him to educate his senior officers in the importance of radio; he demonstrated the speed of communications with the Admiralty, the importance of radio discipline, and how, if a ship breaks silence, she can be identified by the pitch of her morse, even if she only makes one dot. He not only became a radio and radar expert second to none, but was also able to influence the Admiralty in the Typex machines, which were to transform the Navy's entire code and cypher system.

Mountbatten's Combined Operations Headquarters was now at Richmond Terrace, Whitehall, and here he developed a new department of Experiments and Operational Requirements. This enterprise was composed of many large and small components, all of which comprised the vast operation which was to be the invasion of Europe - codenamed Overlord, and here in an office, deep in the basement, I was assigned my own part in the huge jigsaw puzzle.

The varying success of operational raids in Europe had all revealed that we suffered from massive shortages of every sort of craft and equipment, not to mention manpower. Our experience of beach landings had also shown that you cannot capture a heavily defended port without so damaging its facilities as to make it useless. Yet we had to have a sheltered harbour with piers and landing facilities. Thus, the concept of an artificial and prefabricated harbour was born, and the very beginnings of the immortally famous Mulberry (its codename) came from ideas which included floating piers. Churchill wrote an historic memo to Mountbatten: 'They must float up and down with the tide. The anchor problem must be mastered. Let me have the best solution worked out. Don't argue the matter. The difficulties will argue for themselves'.

Although every part of this massive organisation was deadly secret, Mountbatten needed a great deal of technical expertise and advice, and experts of every dimension were accommodated in this labyrinthine headquarters. Brilliant boffins beavered away trying t o solve the many intransigent problems. He had recruited a number of these inventors and geniuses, and Professor Geoffrey Pyke, the wonderfully eccentric scientist, was one of the first. Another memorable character who contributed was Professor Solly Zuckermann, the anatomist and authority on apes, known colloquially as 'The Monkey Man,' having written a book called *The Sex Life of the Primates*, (which became a bestseller among those who supposed it to refer to archbishops!)

In this department, bulging with the finest brains of the day, many ingenious ideas were conceived and planned, and among them the pre-fabricated harbours for the invasion of Normandy. Their construction had to be hidden from enemy reconnaissance aircraft, and this was achieved by building (and temporarily sinking for

175

concealment) each of the 73 concrete and steel caissons, breakwaters, pontoons and floating ramps (for landing vehicles), individually in different ports throughout the UK, to be raised and towed into place for final assembly off the Normandy coast. The most spectacular of these constructions measured sixty by seventeen metres and was the height of a five storey building. The icing on the cake was PLUTO, which was The Pipe Line Under the Ocean from the Isle of Wight to Cherbourg. Eventually there were eleven such pipelines across the Channel which kept pace with our Allied Armies advance inland - according to Bernard Fergusson's *The Watery Maze*.

Perhaps the most unlikely proposition of all of Pyke's inventions was code-named Habakkuk (after an Old Testament prophet of Judah, who lived at the time (c.605 BC), when a Babylonian invasion was imminent). The problem Geoffrey Pyke had been working on was how to protect seaborne landings and Atlantic convoys out of reach of fighter cover; Pyke came up with the ingenious idea of building floating platforms from a mixture of sea water and paper pulp, which frozen together was tougher than steel and would neither melt nor sink, to make a material he called Pykrete, which could be used as seaborne airfields. Both Churchill and Mountbatten were enthusiastic about this concept, and a model was built in Canada. The planned cruising range was about 7000 miles and it would be capable of carrying 200 aircraft. Any damage to the vessel could easily be repaired by pouring in more Pykrete and freezing it.

The moment came when Mountbatten decided to show it off to an interested (if somewhat sceptical) hierarchy - including the Americans, and compare the density of ice with Pykrete. It appears that when all were assembled for the spectacle, Mountbatten used his revolver to fire at the ice, which shattered, but when he fired at the Pykrete his bullet ricocheted round the room, causing considerable alarm - he was not asked for a repeat.

It shows how desperate we were that this frozen construction was considered seriously at all, and incredible that Mulberry was considered the madder of the two ideas. Eventually however, Habakkuk was reluctantly abandoned because as the war progressed we found it less expensive to accept the Portuguese offer of the Azores as a more convenient aircraft carrier.

None of this was known to any of us at the time. Although we observed the frequent visits of our Prime Minister and the mysterious comings and goings of the scientists, it was years later that I realised this was actually the engine house of Overlord and all that was to follow, but we could not fail to feel the sense of urgency in the atmosphere, humming with activity.

My job came under the command of Rear Admiral H E Horan, Landing Craft and Bases (RALB). I was to be working on the actual maps of the planned landings and I was so sworn to secrecy that I never even told John what I had been doing. There were many of us working on individual pieces of the enormous jigsaw, necessary preparations, but none of us knew or ever discussed what the others were doing.

The choice of location on the French coast for our assault was a most sensitive subject and an even more deadly secret than most, because the great debate between the planners, which had been going on for months, (and which had equally obsessed our baffled German enemy), was about where we were going to land - was it to be the Pas de Calais area or the Normandy coast, Baie de la Seine? Once the decision was taken to rule out the fomer, our efforts were concentrated on deceiving the enemy into believing that the Pas de Calais was in fact our main object. The most important element of the deception operation (codenamed Fortitude) was played by the Double Cross agents, whose object was to persuade Hitler that the Normandy landings would be a feint, and that the real assault was to be mounted on the Pas de Calais by a completely fictitious First US Army Group, created with false reports from the Double Cross agents; dummy invasion craft were planted in east coast ports and mobile wireless vehicles travelled round south-east England broadcasting messages from a number of different locations to fool the German radio interception units. We were also dropping bundles of straw to confuse radar reception, which were simulating paratroopers. Bletchley Park was much involved in all this.

The real chosen landing places for the invasion on which my task was based were pinpointed for me on the large scale maps of France in my office, and my particular brief was to delineate everything that could be seen on every compass bearing from each landing position, visible from the bridge of an approaching Landing Craft for identifiable confirmation.

The big scale Ordnance Survey maps were spread out on the wall, and showed railways, roads, churches, castles and every possible feature that would be visible to an incoming invader and from every angle. It was intense and exciting work and obviously vitally important to be detailed and accurate.

This was the beginning of the crescendo to D-Day, and the Senior Commanders and the main offices of Combined Operations - now to be called Allied Expeditionary Force Advance Headquarters - moved from Whitehall, London, to the even more secret location of Southwick House, a mansion near Portsmouth, from where the invasion landings were directed by General Eisenhower, General Montgomery, Air Chief Marshal Tedder and the Allied Naval Commander Admiral Ramsay.

The most favourable date had long been chosen, the tide would be right, but of course the weather - always to be the deciding factor - was bad. All along the south coast of England, 5,400 assault craft with 156,000 men were aboard and at sea waiting for the magic word 'GO'; three million other soldiers, 11,000 aircraft and a trailing procession of vehicles, equipment and armament were holding their breath. If it had to be postponed, the tide would not be right again for another two weeks - how could secrecy be guaranteed? It was Ike's decision, and egged on by Monty it was June 6th and - GO GO GO.

Most Wrens have memories of D-Day, but few have written them down. It was recommended that I write to Lady Rozelle Raynes for a contribution, and in reply she told me of her book, called *Maid Matelot, the Adventures of a Wren Stoker in World War 2, Featuring D Day in Southampton*. 'I was a Wren Stoker', she says, 'on a boat in the Portsmouth Command from 1943-1946, and served with the landing craft at Combined Ops bases before, during and after D-Day. I ended up as a Leading Stoker at the age of 20!....I think you will find everything I remember about my days in the Wrens from those pages'. Here it is: 'It all began on 1st June with all shore leave being cancelled, all phone calls forbidden, no postal service in the Military zone and we should all be confined to barracks at the end of the Royal Pier. Thanks to the army we reached the Royal Pier in double quick time. We passed through the big iron gates and the small iron turnstiles, carrying our mountain of luggage, the gates were firmly locked behind us and that was that. By next day we began to enjoy our enforced imprisonment as the most exciting things in the whole world were taking place in front of our eyes. There was a little black tug called *The Chokka*, which worked from the Royal Pier and spent all day and most of the night helping us with ammunition runs. Most of the landing craft had taken aboard their quota of soldiers, tanks, guns and armoured cars by then and were back on their moorings as sealed ships. No men were allowed ashore and our job was to deliver extra ammunition and urgent signals at all hours of the day and night. I was acting as stoker and deck hand on a new cutter. The wind had been rising all day and heavy showers of driving rain mingled with the flying spindrift; thousands of men sat huddled together under the broad sea-green camouflage nets which covered them and their equipment. There was a pair of Tank Landing Craft, numbers 474 and 7011, moored on B Trot off Netley, and they had not yet been ordered into the hard to load their quota of men and tanks; our Leading Wren was on very friendly terms with the two young lieutenants and late that evening they invited us to come aboard for supper. Some time later we sat down to a banquet of fried eggs, bacon, sausages and baked beans, piled on top of gargantuan slices of fried bread. I had a large sausage poised on the end of a fork half-way between the plate and my mouth, when a bang on the door announced 'Urgent signal just come through Sir - both ships to go into the hard for loading immediately. Then we've got sailing orders for 0600.' For a few brief seconds there was a pregnant silence, and then the two ships burst into rumbustious vibrant life: orders were shouted, heavy boots clattered along the iron decks, engines began to throb, mooring lines were cast off and suddenly we were under way. My dearest wish at that moment was to remain aboard LCT 7011 and take part in the landings on the Normandy coast.

Soldiers and tanks were waiting to be loaded so somehow we were smuggled ashore and back to our quarters. Four hours later I awoke from a dreamless sleep to find someone pouring ice cold water over my face. A signal had just come through from the boat's office to say we were all wanted at Town Quay immediately. 'There are three personnel landing craft broken down somewhere near the Needles' we were told 'and I'm sending you girls down there on *The Chokka* to bring them back. I know that you would all rather stow away on a ship that's bound for France, but the Navy won't allow that so this is the best I can do for you.' All around us the great armada was on the move. There were all the ships we knew so well: the Force Pluto ships from *Abatos*, the infantry landing craft from *Tormentor*, all the hundreds of tank landing craft from Southampton: K Squadron, N Squadron, the Mark Vs and D 15 Flotilla; so many of our favourite ships, all flying barrage balloons, like silver bumble bees sailing amongst fast-moving clouds. Then there were the armed merchant cruisers, destroyers, minesweepers, corvettes, trawlers and ocean tugs, every one of them moving southwards to Normandy and a fate unknown.'

Very special Boating Wrens were trained to serve as pilots on D-Day: here is what Wren Lita C Edwards has to say in *The Wren* magazine, 1961. 'Shortly after D-Day I was ordered to take two boats out into the Solent to meet a disabled LCI(S) (Landing Ship Infantry) and tow her into the Hamble river. When we found the ship, she was already being towed by a sister ship, but another LCI(S), No 353, was down at Gosport sinking - could we do something about her? She was lying with her bow completely under the water, and propellers and rudders high in the air. My other boat arrived so we lashed one boat on each side of 353 as far aft as possible and started to tow her stern first....I took my stand on the highest part where I could be seen by both boats and, by our own code of visual signals, I could control the speed of both boats. After some three hours towing we got within sight of the base, and I asked the CO to call up the signal station and asked to have the jetty cleared for us, and the big fire pumps standing by. When we got into the river it seemed to us that the whole ship's company, from the Captain down, was waiting for us. When we put her on the hard at high water we could see what was wrong. She had a hole 11 feet long in the bottom, under the troop compartment, received when she ran into an underwater stake on the Normandy beaches.

Three days later 353 was off once more to France, and our reward was her CO's remark that he did not care what happened to him in the future, whatever it was the WRNS would see him through'.

This account, bubbling with enthusiasm, written in the pregnant days preceding D-Day when we were all sealed into whatever job we were doing, is from Ex Leading Wren Jean Cochrane:

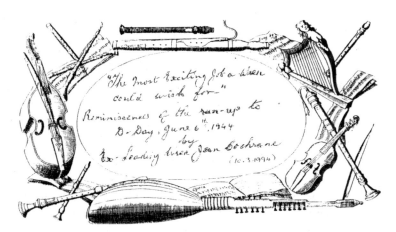

'The Most Exciting Job a Wren Could Wish For.
Reminiscences of the run-up to D-Day.'

'I had been sent to the Nore Holding Depot at Rochester, Kent after my request for a change from my job as a Topographical Wren at Oxford, where I had been posted for just over a year. I had volunteered in 1942 and time was passing. Although I had enjoyed my time in Oxford, working on a top secret job alongside members of the Admiralty as well as WRNS, I had begun to feel that somehow I was not really in the Navy! So there I was in the Dickensian cathedral town of Rochester, certainly full of Naval activity, being so close to Chatham Barracks. I loved the atmosphere, the hustle and bustle of sailors and Wrens passing through. Squad Drill every morning, (not everyone's cup of tea!) but I enjoyed it.

I had had a chat with the Officer-in-Charge, then a Second Officer Burtenshaw, whose job it was to choose suitable drafts for Wrens passing through her hands. In the meantime I was occupied by a variety of duties. On one occasion I received a message: 'Would you please teach the Wrens this song'! As I was a music student, this was an agreeable task and one I hope I performed satisfactorily - it was a song full of patriotic feelings, of European flavour and went with a swing.

One day I received an order to report to the Officer in Charge, WRNS, and accordingly found myself again in the presence of Second Officer Burtenshaw. This time she addressed me very directly and said: 'Cochrane I have sent for you as I have been requested to handpick Wrens for a job - I cannot tell you anything about the job and it may not be exactly what you had in mind, but I can assure you that if you accept it you will never regret it. I want you to think about it very carefully and let me know what you decide.'

'Needless to say, the next morning I informed Second Officer Burtenshaw that I was quite prepared to take on the mysterious job, at which she seemed pleased, and subsequently I was drafted to London.

The WRNS quarters were very comfortable indeed, being in the buildings in Prince's Gate, Kensington; all had been commandeered for the Wrens. The place of work was not so luxurious - there being hardly any furniture apart from the bare necessities - such as a desk, a chair and a filing cabinet or two. The location was Ashley Gardens in the vicinity of Westminster Cathedral, near Victoria. We were not told very much initially about our work, but I do remember being told that I was now BIGOT and all our papers etc were so stamped. This I later understood was even more Secret than Top Secret. As far as I can remember, the three months we spent in Ashley Gardens revealed no definite plan of work for me - I hardly saw any officers or indeed fellow Wrens - in fact it was all very mysterious.

Then one day we we re told we we re 'on the move' - it was goodbye to dear old Prince's Gate and down to the South of England. Things were beginning to happen, there was something in the air....and we were in the thick of things. We now realised that we were part of Naval Command Eastern Task Force, headed by Admiral Sir Philip Vian, formerly known as Vian of the *Cossack* for his bravery in boarding the *Altmark* in the Norwegian Fjord, and all the Wrens now became aware of the duties they were to perform.

I myself found that I was in the Operations Room with no other Wren, and the room was full of highpowered and talented Naval officers. In the centre of the room was a huge billiard-like table, on the edge of which, in one corner, Yours Truly sat! This table was the only one available for the Staff Navigating Officer to lay out his plans, charts and maps etc, and he made it quite clear, in the nicest possible way, just how much or little space he was prepared to allow me and I certainly knew it if I strayed over my boundaries. I was seated directly behind my Officer, who was the Senior Staff Officer and responsible for Operations, known for short as S.O.O. He worked very hard and I do not think he ever took a break; he was a silent man completely engrossed in his work. He passed all the signals over to me or left them in my In-tray if I was out to lunch, and I duly kept a chart on which the movement of every ship, Landing Craft, MTB, Minesweeping Vessel or whatever, which would constitute our Invasion Fleet, was recorded from day to day, including the movement of Force 'S' from the North of Scotland.

Of course I was not allowed to talk about my job to anyone, not even other Wrens working for NCETF, so it was rather a lonely business, but I did not mind that - I knew I was doing a unique job which mattered.

My proudest moment came when, one day, on coming back from lunch, I found Robin (S.O.O.) with a visiting officer, patiently standing by my place at the table corner, waiting for me, and he gently asked: 'Wren Cochrane, may we have a look at your chart, please?' 'Certainly Sir' I answered, delighted, and quickly produced my handiwork - and there was a complete picture of every ship in the Invasion Fleet, neatly berthed in Portsmouth Harbour, according to plan, and ready to take the personnel on board to set them on the Normandy Beaches; my task was completed and now all that remained was to set sail.

We were at Fort Southwick overlooking Portsmouth Harbour (WRNS Quarters were at the Naval Air Station, Fareham) and there was a buzz of activity all around with important people like Eisenhower and Monty in the offing. No-one was allowed to leave the perimeter, and Wrens were taken to and from their quarters by special Navy buses. Of course there was a decided air of excitement, and soon it was apparent that D-Day was imminent.

I searched, in common with the other NCETF Wrens, for a 'Good Luck' 4 leafed clover to give to my Commander, Cdr Robin Maurice,

S.O.O., NCETF on the eve of the departure for Normandy. To my great joy and relief I found one, and duly and somewhat shyly presented it to S.O.O. who received it with quite a show of surprised pleasure, and I felt good about that.

The next morning on arriving at Fort Southwick, I looked over the familiar scene of Portsmouth Harbour - not a ship was to be seen, nor a single serviceman - all had set sail for Normandy and the rest is history. Before long, I too set sail for France, and later was one of the first of the Wrens to enter Germany.

P.S. I should have liked to have had an opportunity of thanking Second Officer Burtenshaw for giving me a job which I certainly will never forget and which gave me a *raison d'être* during the 1940-45 War years, before returning to my musical training at the Royal Academy of Music.'

Anne Heathcote (now Baroness van Lynden of The Hague, Holland), in spite of describing herself as a 'self-confessed deserter', had a very responsible job working for a most distinguished Brigadier Viscount Head, one of the most important people in Mountbatten's Combined Operations team, and one of Montgomery's right-hand men. It is a coincidence that sixty years ago Anne and I were both working there in the same division without knowing it, during the desperate days culminating in D-Day, and only now do I discover it. Perhaps we did meet?

Anne begins: 'When I joined the WRNS aged eighteen and a half I was lucky enough to form, almost immediately, a threesome with Maria Monckton (now Chaworth Musters) and Florence Lloyd. I remember our first evening in Portsmouth watching with amazement, from top bunks next to each other, as our mates put on thick pyjamas over their corsets, stockings, vests and bras and got into bed.

The three of us were sent at our request to Weymouth, Maria and Florence to be plotters and I with a secretarial course behind me, to be secretary to the Engineer Officer at Weymouth Harbour, HMS *Bee*, a working up base for coastal forces MGBs, MTBs. My boss, a Lieutenant Commander, owned a garage in Ilfracombe and the other officers and men were all motor mechanics. It was easy work and quite fun, the flotillas of boats came in for a week or more of training. Occasionally I was taken out on one of the boats, although it was strictly forbidden; Wren ratings were not supposed to go to the Wardroom.

My boss was very dark and quite attractive. He had a wife in Ilfracombe of whom he was jealous, and always went on leave with a revolver in case he found her *en flagrante*. I thought she might have some excuse as he always used to dictate his letters to her. Deadly dull they were. I thought this very strange and resolved never to marry a man who might send me dictated letters.

I worked in the boss's office on the quay which was always crowded with officers from the boats begging for attention for their delicate motors. I suppose I did do some typing, but all I remember was an enormous amount of chat.

The Wrenery was in an ex boys' boarding school, not uncomfortable; the baths, perhaps six, were all in a row in a downstairs bathroom. We used to tiptoe in and turn on the lights to disperse the carpet of cockroaches and then, those of us who were into baths wallowed and gossiped in the lovely steamy warmth.

When the south coast was being prepared for the invasion, 1943-44, HMS *Bee* was moved to Holyhead on Anglesey. I was billeted in a dirty house, put in the sheets of the previous Wren and during the three or four weeks I was there, the wind was never in the right direction for there to be any hot water. I hated Holyhead and begged my boss to have me moved. I dare say he was quite glad to get rid of me. Anyway, in a very short time I found myself a Naval Cadet at Greenwich.

I got into trouble at Greenwich. I acquired from somewhere a bottle of gin, then in short supply, and hitchhiked to London to give it to my mother. But I was spotted, had up before a top Wren and was assured that officers did not hitchhike, especially not when openly carrying a bottle of gin. However I passed out successfully and was appointed to Combined Operations in Whitehall.

It was a lovely job. I lived comfortably at home, the work was not at all onerous or difficult and the ambience so civilised I loved it. I worked in the office of the Joint Planner, Brigadier Head, who became Minister of Defence in a post war cabinet. I shared the office with a very pretty and sympathetic ATS Officer, Jean Chopping, and a competent ATS shorthand typist who did all the real work.

The minutes of the Chiefs of Staff committee came to us daily, plus many of the War Cabinet, several copies of e a ch. Our job was to d eposit the information in these papers into as many files as we could think of, so that there would be a complete dossier on any subject the Brigadier might ask for. We spent our days cutting up these minutes and papers and sticking them in files - it was extremely secret which is why there had to be officers doing it. I am by nature quite indiscreet, but never once during the war did I have the slightest temptation to tell anyone about the information that I encountered.

We knew all about D-Day and agonized about the last minute build up of German troops behind Caen, which we could see on the big wall map in the operations room. I remember praying until my knees hurt. A quite separate memory I have is of a V-bomb going off one Sunday morning when I was on duty - the bang seemed to be in line with Buckingham Palace - at just 11.30, I prayed again that it hadn't hit the Guards Chapel, but it had.

After D-Day, when we were struggling to retake France, the Dutch Prime Minister told Churchill that if Holland was not liberated by May, the Dutch nation might never rise again. People were starving, the railways weren't working, the situation was desperate. I went in to see Brigadier Head with this piece of news. 'Something must be done about this' I said, 'I am going to marry my Dutchman in May'.

Perhaps as a result of this outburst, when I came back from our week's honeymoon I found I had lost my job. I was now a registered alien and it was against regulations that I should do such secret work. They offered me another job in the Press Department, but I was so cross, especially as my husband (a Dutch Naval Officer who had escaped to Britain from a German prisoner of war camp in 1944) was at that moment in a British destroyer on a convoy to Malta, that I deserted. 'Win the war yourselves' I thought to myself and went happily to Liverpool where my husband's destroyer was due to dock. Months later I was sent a letter of appreciation, a sum of money and some very welcome clothing coupons. I had had an unexciting, unheroic but happy time in the Wrens.'

Technically Wrens couldn't really desert as we were never made to sign the Naval Discipline Act, so Anne's honourable discharge seems to me assured.

CHAPTER 24

───── ⚓ ─────

VICTORY IN SIGHT

You might think that after the tremendous drama of D-Day, the aftermath could be something of an anticlimax. But the enormous activity continued day and night. Reinforcements and supplies were vital, casualties came back to be treated in hospital, damaged vehicles and vessels returned for repair. Communications by teleprinter, telephone and radio went on relentlessly. As soon as possible organisations were set up in France, and Wrens played their full part crossing the Channel and replacing men.

The Hon Maria Monckton (Chaworth Musters), one of the three-some of friends, adds this story of what happened to her after the invasion:

Maria was a Plotting Wren based at Immingham, which covered the area from the Humber down to the Wash. 'We worked 24 hours a day in watches, 8am-2pm, 2pm-8pm and 8am-8pm. The Plotting table was covered in a very large scale map of our area and we moved ships and convoys so that our officers could see what was happening. The Plotting Officers north and south of us kept us informed of the shipping movements which concerned us; if it was a convoy, how many ships it was composed of, and the number of single ships with their direction and speed. We also received information from the local RAF Radar stations who gave us map references every half hour and checked numbers of ships in convoy - if there were U-boats about, it was important to know if any ships were missing.'

After D-Day it was a natural progression for some of our local plots to be transferred to Europe, and Maria describes her emigration to Ostend in November of that year:

Maria (left),
Naval Party 1764,
Ramsgate-Ostend

15 November 1944: 'We had the most hectic day. At 9 o'clock we trotted off to report to First Officer who gave us a pep-talk and then hustled us into a bus which was waiting outside. This was the first time we had all met and everyone clung nervously to the people they already knew. It's difficult now to remember what one's first impressions were, as we have lived and worked together for so long that we know the best and the worst of each other only too well, but jogging up to London in the bus on that first day I felt I'd never be clever enough to keep up with all the rest. Everyone kept up an incessant chatter as we bumped along on our wooden utility seats, except for those who were inclined to be sick and so sat silently in the front row, while the rest of us decided to have our hair permed (in case it rained a lot and we had to live in a tent), or meet our families or buy some thick pyjamas or even have a last good meal.

We eventually arrived at our destination, where we were fed and then removed to the store where we were fitted up. This consisted of giving us a kit bag, various articles of clothing suitable for winter wear at the North Pole, a water bottle, some tin 'mess traps' (plates, knives, forks etc), 24 hour rations, tommy cookers, and finally a huge valise complete with camp bed, canvas bucket, chair and bath. These took at least two people to move, but we eventually managed to move them into our bus, which we then patted on the back and despatched to the Depot. Meanwhile we went our separate ways, did our last minute things and then returned exhausted and rather miserable, to our last night (or so we thought) in England.'

16 November 1944: 'We were called at 0400 this morning, and after much shivering and disappearing under the bedclothes, we managed to get up and dress, packed our toothbrushes and pyjamas and started off. As we tiptoed downstairs in the day, the siren went off outside and the whole thing became so terribly eerie that we simply flew down the last few steps and tore outside, where sou'westers and hairnets (as nothing is worse for our hair and therefore our morale, as rain at the beginning of the day). Everything being under control we put our luggage on the barrow and set off to the other house, to find the rest of the party and some breakfast; this turned out to be the most awful struggle as the rain put the torch out, and the barrow squeaked to such an extent we feared the whole population would turn out to see if we were committing a murder in the street. Fortunately they must have become hardened to the behaviour of the services in their midst, and we arrived complete with luggage just in time for breakfast which we gobbled up. We then plodded outside again into the rain to load the bus and pile ourselves in.

At last we started, and after picking up the last few stragglers and their belongings, (which included bicycles) we left Chatham behind us and set off for Ramsgate. As we jolted along, the darkness began gradually to lift and we could see the villages that we passed, though even they looked dingy and drab with rain pouring down and the leafless trees bending and twisting in the wind. We arrived quite safely and went off to have a look round. Having sent a PC of the pier home and drunk a rather tepid and disgusting cup of tea, we returned to the bus only to be told that it was much too rough to sail and that we had got to go back to the Depot and wait till tomorrow. So back we went, and spent the afternoon at the pictures, going early to bed to get strength enough to repeat the day's performance.'

17 November 1944: 'The first few hours today were much the same as yesterday's, though luckily the rain had stopped as had some of the wind, so when we arrived in Ramsgate we found everyone ready to sail. We drove for what seemed like miles along the top of the breakwater, sitting in the bus and looking down at the sea almost underneath us, trying not to move in case the whole thing toppled over; no disaster occurred and we found the ML (Motor Launch) at the very end of the breakwater waiting for us, so we descended very gingerly, climbed down a little ladder and embarked. Our luggage was thrown down after us, causing the boats to sink at least six more inches; we were then battened down below, the boats cast off and away we sailed. The only disappointment of the whole day were the White Cliffs, which owing to the foulness of the weather weren't even white, and which disappeared from view before we had been allowed up on deck, so no romantic memories of them for us.

We had the most heavenly trip. A corvette was lying at anchor just outside Ramsgate that signalled 'Good Luck' to us; from there we did not see another ship till we were more than halfway over and met the convoys coming back. We soon left them behind and began to get nearer to Belgium. Maisie and I spent our time on the bridge longing to be the first to see the coastline, staring through the glasses until we could almost see mountains coming out of the sea. When one of the officers pointed and said 'There it is!', neither of us could see a thing, though we both shrieked 'Yes!' with one breath, hoping it didn't sound too false. Then we did see a dark line on the horizon and gradually houses on the front, after which we were pushed below again, and next time we were allowed up we were right inside Ostende harbour. The whole place seemed to be a shambles - on each side the wharves had been blown up, with twisted bits of steel left behind - even so the place was a hive of industry. There were merchantmen tied up wherever there was space, and where we came alongside in the Coastal Force Base it was humming with activity.

The effect when they all saw us was quite the funniest thing, as every single person stopped working and stood with their mouths open gaping at us - they had every reason to, for an odder collection of people would be hard to imagine. We were all wearing trousers and were festooned like Christmas trees with the more portable of our belongings; it had been a fairly rough crossing so no-one was really looking their best. However, we managed to keep our heads, and scramble up the little ladder on to dry land, where we were at once pushed into a lorry and driven off to Navy House. It was about 1600 hrs by then and they must have thought we hadn't had a meal that day. We were led off to the Wardroom, told where to sit, and the most enormous plates piled high with stew and potatoes were put in front of us. (Nothing worse could possibly have happened as one or two people weren't feeling awfully well on the boat, and Maisie and I, under the impression that there was no food at all on the continent, had eaten six people's rations on the way over). After hours of swallowing and drinking, and drinking and swallowing again we finished, heaving sighs of relief, only to find ourselves face to face with another plate, this time with 16 prunes each. This was the final straw, and we became rather hysterical trying to encourage the few who liked prunes to eat 176 between them.

We were then removed from the table, put into the lorry and taken to the Blackpool Hotel, which was to be our new home. It isn't very difficult to imagine how thrilled we were when we saw it as we had been expecting to live in a trench, sleeping in the open on our camp beds and living on our 24 hour rations, instead of which we had enormous comfortable beds, two in each room, delicious food for every meal and the whole house belonging to us. It didn't seem as if it could be true.

Plotting in Ostend was, however, very different. Radar was in its infancy and the stations needed to be on very high ground to function properly, and unfortunately behind Ostend the terrain was completely and utterly flat. So at night when the German E-boats, still operating from Dunkirk, came close in searching for our MTBs (Motor Torpedo Boats) and Gun Boats and fought them, we could see through the window when their guns fired - and even hear their voices - but no way could the radar pick them up. Soon after this they surrendered, and we went to Dunkirk and saw their midget submarines.

German Midget Submarines off Dunkirk

When VE-day came we had a Victory Parade through Ostend, and then with a great deal of excitement went home and worked in a factory in Slough while we waited to be demobbed.'

CHAPTER 25

——— ⚓ ———

STORNOWAY AND OUT

The last year of my Wren life was as interesting and unexpected as the rest of it. Our fate was always in the hands of their Lordships of the Admiralty, and as John had survived almost everything the Atlantic could throw at him, he was allowed a respite from the violence of the elements and the enemy and appointed to a 'working up centre', suitably named HMS *Mentor*. This was to be found at Stornoway, the principal town of the Isle of Lewis in the Hebrides, about as far as you can get from civilisation; it was not however beset with enemy action - as yet - and therefore might be called peaceful. His relief, who arrived in Falmouth to take over *Oribi*, wanted to do the handover at sea. *Oribi* was ordered to Scapa Flow, which meant an amazing 2,000 mile non-stop journey for John - from Kirkwall to Inverness by air, then from Inverness to London and on to Falmouth by train. I had some leave, so we travelled back together to London, to Inverness, then to Kyle of Lochalsh and finally by steamer to Stornoway - almost as far as you can go in the UK.

The object of his activities would be to train Reserve and Hostilities Only officers who were to command the large numbers of new escorts now being commissioned, how to organise, handle and run their ships and work them up, ready for action as convoy escorts. Stornowegians are a unique race who are mostly *Wee Frees* - a minority of the Free Church, which refused to join the United Free Church in 1900. Their religion interferes with their lives and everyone else's. On a Sunday, for instance, any sort of activity is breaking the Sabbath - writing a letter, bicycling, even gardening; such hobbies were deeply disapproved of, and disapproval could result in dismissal from accommodation. One Naval officer publicly proclaimed himself a Jew so he could continue with his weekend gardening. John noticed on his walk to Matins at the Episcopal Church of Scotland, that all the blinds would still be drawn mid morning in the houses by the roadside and were still undrawn on his return. They would only be opened in time for evening service at the Free Kirk. John suspected - cynically - that the cause of this was not so much religious enthusiasm but more the result of very hard drinking on the previous Saturday night.

Having decided to try my hand at being a housewife, I found a small flat to rent and set about some cooking. My life so far had not even included boiling an egg, so I managed to borrow a cookery book from one of the destroyers which gave a variety of recipes for steak and kidney pudding, plum duff, and other Naval favourites. Unfortunately they were all intended to feed 240 men, and it was difficult to work out a suitable proportion for a modest two. After a good deal of division I decided not to try both at once, but to have a go at the steam pudding, having started the meal with kippers - which were the staple diet at all meals in Stornoway and did not require much culinary skill. When I had bought the required ingredients I mixed them up as instructed, and allowing what I supposed was enough room for it to rise, I wrapped it up in a vest (ex-Wren issue, surplus to requirements) and put it in a large saucepan to boil and started to read my book. What I hadn't grasped from the Naval cookery book was how long to allow this much divided pudding, so I left it on until kipper time, thinking the rather unattractive looking gluey lump would be better for overcooking than under. When the moment came, I was quite unable to tell if it was cooked or not; I had a feeling it was supposed to rise or alter in some way, but it looked much the same as when I had put it in. I gave some to John, who luckily seemed to think it was cooked and ate quite a lot, remarking that it was good and filling. Another recipe I had rather forced on me by the butcher was when he kindly gave me a sheep's head, which was not only without coupons but free. My heart sank as I read the cookery instructions: 'remove the brains and tongue!' (it didn't seem to have eyes - thank God!) - I persevered. 'Soak it for 12 hours, changing the water repeatedly. Boil it for 4 hours, add some veg and herbs, reboil it for 2 hours - it was still grinning at me and every saucepan in the kitchen was now covered in a sort of green slime; further suggestions: 'the brains can be used for brain cakes' (that's tea taken care of), and 'only a small portion of the head need be served in the broth, the rest can be served separately with the tongue and brain sauce'. This should have lasted us for a week, but just as we were about to taste the first morsel, I began to feel quite hysterical when I suddenly remembered its teeth! Oh, for M & S ready-cooked meals!

John, meanwhile, was having great trouble with his training courses. The local Laird insisted on having only his local countrymen as his crew, and communicating with them from the bridge exclusively in Gaelic. By the time he had interpreted to John what he was telling them to do and John had told him that his orders would result in catastrophe, the crew had grown rather bored and started fishing.

Another of the jobs John took on was Recruiting Officer for the Hebrides, when the proper officer had gone sick. When called up, all the young men of the island opted for the Navy and were accepted on principle. Knowing however, from personal experience, that all the superb Hebridean seamen-fishermen had long since been absorbed into the Service and were serving in trawlers, these men now being called up were from inland crofts, knew nothing about the sea and were too slow to learn, so John sent them all into the Army. An irate Major came all the way from Scottish Command to remonstrate!

HMS Broadway

After this not wholly successful sojourn in Stornoway, John was appointed to his first command, HMS *Broadway*. He was ecstatic with joy and described her as 'a typical flush deck, four stacker, a 'cow' in a seaway and with a turning circle like a battleship, but beauty is in the eye of the beholder and she was my very own'.

Well, I realised I had to take second place after that and must do something to regain my position. It seemed a convenient moment to announce that I was going to have a baby, not only to restore my prestige but also to be able to retire from the WRNS on one of the few grounds over which their Lordships of the Admiralty had no control.

I found us another flat near Inverkeithing with a superb view of the Forth rail bridge. *Broadway* spent her time patrolling up and down the North sea, and on every occasion of entering or leaving harbour she had to pass in full view of and quite close to our house.

Me with my firstborn child, Felicity Anne

Thus, a simple pre-arranged signal - a bucket hoisted to the Crow's Nest momentarily on a halyard - signified that he would be home for the next meal. What those meals consisted of I have happily no recollection - all I do remember was the terrible day when I inadvertently dropped our fortnightly egg.

So although I left the Wrens at this point, life was going to continue to be as it had been over the four tumultuous years of war. I had grown up considerably, fed on this rather exotic diet of plunging head-first into one unknown job after another. Now I had taken on with complete but quite unjustified confidence, a lifelong commitment of being a sailor's wife, and the prospect of this baby. But for us ex-Wrens who had discovered independence and freedom, the world was now our oyster, and when John was sent out to Hong Kong in command of an Algerine minesweeper, HMS *Moon*, shortly after our daughter Felicity Anne

HMS Moon - how John earned his nickname 'The Man in the Moon'

was born, I thought nothing of blowing everything in my bank and following the Fleet. It was just after the war had ended, and John had sent me a signal telling me to get to Gibraltar any way I could. It was at our own expense in those days, but I found a Dakota - that immortal, ubiquitous, maid-of-all-work aeroplane - which went via Lisbon, and I arrived plus baby, landing on that hair-raising airfield of Gibraltar, where his ship HMS *Moon* was to be refitted.

I will never forget the thrill of getting out of poor war-ravaged England in this wonderful machine. Finding no-one to meet me (a many times repeated situation I soon learned to take in my stride), I went penniless straight to the Rock Hotel where Felicity Anne and I lived on bananas and ginger biscuits - both unknown in England since the war began - until rescued by other members of the flotilla, HMS *Mary Rose* and HMS *Seabear* - and finally by John, 'the Man in the Moon', as he was known.

But that, as they say, is another story.

INDEX

ULTRA 120
Uprichard, Chief Officer
WRNS 98

Vaughan, Rosemary 124, 125
Vian, Admiral Sir Philip 182
Vidette, HMS 78

Watson Watt, Mr 124
Welby, Mrs, Superintendent
WRNS 39
Western Approaches 66, 164–5,
plotting for 40–1
Western Desert Force 46, 69,
71–2
Weymouth 185
Whale Island Gunnery School
97
Whitehead (Ford), Norrice 64–5,
67
Wilhelmsburg, German steamer
47
Winchester, Flowerdown 123–6
Winn, Captain Rodger 165
Woodstock, HMS 112
WRNS (Women's Royal Naval
Service) 15–16
categories of employment 16,
25–7, 92
Headquarters 7, 8–10
interviews and medical for
3–4, 139
Leading Wren badge *19*
Officer Selection 32–8
popularity of 8, 9, 16, 29–30

service at sea 109–19, 154
social mix 5–6, 29–30, 84–5,
89–90, 129–30
training 4–7, 29, 30
uniform 3, 8, 9–10, 30–1
wartime casualties 16–18
Wynn Jones, Mary, Wren
Steward 34–8

Y Service, Naval Intelligence 121

Zuckermann, Professor Solly
175

207